High King of Heaven

Also published by Cistercian Publications

By the same author:

The Venerable Bede (new edition 1998)

The Harlots of the Desert: A Study of Repentance in Early Monastic Sources (1987)

The World of the Desert Fathers (Fairacres Press 1986)

The Sayings of the Desert Fathers (1975)

CISTERCIAN STUDIES SERIES:
NUMBER ONE HUNDRED EIGHTY-ONE

HIGH KING OF HEAVEN

Aspects of Early English Spirituality

Benedicta Ward SLG

CISTERCIAN PUBLICATIONS
Kalamazoo, Michigan – Spencer, Massachusetts

13545

Published in Great Britain by Mowbray,
a Cassell imprint

Cistercian Publications
Editorial Offices: WMU Station, Kalamazoo, Michigan 49008
Distribution: St Joseph's Abbey, Spencer, Massachusetts 01562

First published 1999

Library of Congress Cataloging in Publication Data
is available on request.

ISBN 0 87907 581 3 (hardback)
0 87907 781 6 (paperback)

Extracts from Bede, *Ecclesiastical History of the English People*,
ed. and trans. B. Colgrave and R. A. B. Mynors (1969)
are reprinted by permission of Oxford University Press.

Cover picture: Christ in Majesty, Add. MS 49598.70. Used by permission
of The British Library.

Typeset by SetSystems, Saffron Walden, Essex
Printed and bound in Great Britain by
Biddles Ltd, Guildford and King's Lynn

The work of Cistercian Publications is made possible
in part by support from Western Michigan University
to The Institute of Cistercian Studies

Contents

Illustrations

The bishops worship at St Alban's tomb and pray for his help against the Pelagians. From the Book of St Albans, TCD MS 177, fol. 54r.
By permission of The Board of Trinity College Dublin.

Sea creatures minister to St Cuthbert after a night praying in the sea. From Bede's Life of St Cuthbert, University College MS 165, p. 35.
By permission of The Master and Fellows of University College, Oxford.

Guthlac attacked by demons. Harley Roll no. Y6, seventh roundel.
By permission of The British Library.

Guthlac and St Bartholomew with demons. Harley Roll no. Y6, eighth roundel.
By permission of The British Library.

Cast of the Ruthwell Cross, Dumfriesshire, on display in Durham Cathedral. A cast of the Bewcastle Cross, from Cumbria, is visible in the background.
© Department of Archaeology, University of Durham. Photographer T. Middlemass.
Used with permission.

For my friends, pupils and colleagues

I direct others to the shore of perfection while I am still tossing on the waves of transgression. But I beg you, in this shipwreck of my life, hold me up with the plank of your prayers, so that while my own heaviness makes me sink, the hands of your goodness may lift me up.

(Gregory the Great, *Pastoral Care*, Book IV)

Preface

In an article which he wrote in 1907, entitled with typical modesty 'About an Old Prayer Book', Edmund Bishop prefaced his comments by referring to what he called

> a subject deeply, vitally interesting and yet I fancy little known and less considered, viz. the history and vicissitudes of what I may call English piety.[1]

The following pages are an attempt to follow up the 'deeply, vitally interesting' subject, in discussing aspects of the devotional life of the Anglo-Saxons in England in the first years after their conversion, i.e. the seventh and eighth centuries. The discussion is necessarily selective and concentrates mainly on the Latin texts of prayers, corporate and individual, with some reference to later texts in Anglo-Saxon and also to non-literary sources. It contains little mention of early Romano-British or of Welsh Christianity, not because they are unimportant in themselves but because they had little effect on the main line of English spirituality in this period. Moreover, with a large subject, one has to draw the line somewhere.

Two other explanations should be given here about the title and scope of this book. It is about the 'English' rather than the 'Anglo-Saxon', since the latter term is perhaps misleading in that it may suggest a contrast with 'Celtic'. It seems to me that these terms are best understood by relationship rather than by contrast. There is at present an idea that early English Christianity involved triumphalist Roman missionaries in conflict with the simple Celts, British and Irish, a situation Edmund Bishop noted nearly a hundred years ago:

> Some persons will hear only of what is 'British'; and others ... will have it that we are Anglo-Celts not Anglo-Saxons ...

He went on to underline their essential unity when he wrote:

> In the devotional products of the first period ... the Irishman and the Roman are pouring their respective pieties into the devoted isle and we absorb both kinds; but the English mind and religious sense assert themselves in the process of fusion and contribute to the resultant a quality and measure possessed by neither Celt nor Roman alone ... I seem to discern as the specifically 'English' quality of this earliest devotional literature, strong feeling controlled and also penetrated by good sense.[2]

I have not written about Celtic, Roman or Anglo-Saxon but about the mingling of these which produced English piety, stressing the mixture rather than the ingredients.

Secondly, it may also be necessary to define here what I mean by the term 'spirituality', like 'Celtic' a word so widely used now as to mean, to quote Humpty Dumpty, 'what I choose it to mean'. 'Spirituality' is not a word Anglo-Saxons, Celts or Romans would have recognized, nor indeed is it, in its modern sense, a medieval word at all. Its earlier use was in the plural, 'spiritualities', referring to spiritual jurisdiction as opposed to temporal jurisdiction, the 'lords spiritual' as opposed (and how often literally opposed!) to the 'lords temporal'. 'Spiritualité' has of course undergone a later transformation and in French there is a very good chance that 'un spirituel' will be someone who is witty, lively, or even mad. These are not the uses of the word I have in mind when I write about the spirituality of the Anglo-Saxons. There is another use of the word 'spirituality' nowadays (which I also regard with caution, since it seems vaguely gnostic), in which it means the non-material aspect of things, as in the 'spirituality of nature', 'the spirituality of progress', 'the spirituality of electronics', a passive use of the phrase, referring, I hope, to human reaction to these objects. A more active use of the phrase is current in 'the spirituality of Islamic culture', and this is closer to the use I want to make of the term. To see the desires and religious aspirations of men within their cultural context can be extremely illuminating, especially in connection with non-literate societies. I prefer to combine this modern use of the word 'spirituality' (which is perhaps closer to 'mentality') with another meaning given to it in the nineteenth century when it was coined. It was used then to describe a field of study earlier called ascetic theology, and/or mystical prayer. By 'spirituality', then, I mean what the Anglo-Saxons thought and said and did and prayed in the light of the Gospel of Christ. This in turn has its limitation in that it is not possible to explore the deepest centre of such a relationship; there is, as Thomas Merton wrote,

> a point of pure truth (at the centre of our being), a point or spark which belongs entirely to God, which is never at our disposal, from which God disposes our lives, which is inaccessible to the fantasies of our mind or the brutalities of our own will.[3]

I have therefore presented some of the outward reflections of this inner depth, where there is evidence for this in these very distant times. I make no apology for the fact that much of the material available is found in the life and works of the Venerable Bede, since he was both an articulate Anglo-Saxon himself, the greatest recorder of the conversion of any barbarian people, and a major formative influence on the tradition through his own writings.

I would like to thank my community for their interest and help, and especially Sister Christine SLG. I am deeply indebted to many friends and colleagues for discussion of this field over many years, especially to Bishop Rowan Williams, Professor Eamonn O'Carragain, Dr Santha Bhattacharji, Mr Nigel Frith, Professor S. Bradley, Professor Henry Mayr-Harting, Dr A. M. Allchin, Dr Oliver Nicolson, and many more. I am surrounded by a great cloud of witnesses, in which this book is part of a lively and ongoing exploration.

Notes

1   Edmund Bishop, *Liturgica Historica* (Oxford, 1917), p. 385.

2   Ibid.

3   Thomas Merton, *Conjectures of a Guilty Bystander* (London, 1965), p. 142.

Abbreviations

CCSL	Corpus Christianorum, Series Latina
EHEP	Bede, *Ecclesiastical History of the English People*
HA	Bede, *Lives of the Abbots of Wearmouth and Jarrow*
PL	*Patrologia Latina*, ed. J.–P. Migne
VSC	Bede, *Life of St Cuthbert*

1

Mediterranean influences

'To teach by word and example'

It was to Rome that the English looked for the source of their knowledge of the Gospel. This had always been the case in the island of Britain when it had been part of the Roman empire, when knowledge of Christianity was brought along with the legions from Christians in Rome and Gaul. The heretic Pelagius had been British, the first Christian emperor, Constantine, had been proclaimed at York, and the martyrdom of Alban had given the British Church the essential sign of the cross over human life to the end. There are, however, few literary records of the first Christians in Britain[1] and it is in accounts of the reception of Christianity by the barbarian Anglo-Saxon occupiers of the island in the sixth century that the basis of English spirituality can be seen to have been laid down.

Christianity came to them in two ways: by the missionaries sent by Pope Gregory I from Rome and by the Irish missionaries who owed their Christianity similarly to Rome. The chief architect of the mission from Rome was Gregory the Great and the character and gifts of this man marked English spirituality permanently. Gregory had such a special care for the English that Bede called him 'our apostle'. Bede's love of Gregory was partly because he sent Augustine and his companions to begin the conversion of the Anglo-Saxons in 597, partly because Gregory also was a monk, partly that as an author Bede owed a great deal to the writings of Gregory but perhaps also because Gregory's writings were forged in the furnace of disaster and pain, both general and personal.

Gregory was called by Bede one of the four great Latin fathers of the Church, and the tone of his writings, as well as his personal advice to the English mission, was a main strand in early English spirituality.

Gregory[2] was born about 540, son of a noble senatorial family. His parents were Christian and two of his aunts were nuns; he himself became a monk. When he was 38, he was sent as an ambassador by the Pope to Constantinople, and twelve years later he was made Pope. At heart Gregory always defined himself as a monk and man of prayer; he wrote the life of St Benedict and commended his *Rule* for monks. His writings greatly influenced the vocabulary of prayer of the Latin West and are among the formative mystical writings of the Church. Gregory was one of the busiest men in Christendom. However much he lamented his loss of silence and solitude and mourned his inability to cope with affairs, his Roman sense of civic duty, combined with his suppleness in the hands of God to whom he had totally committed his life, caused him to undertake enormously difficult tasks since they were asked of him. There was the practical care of the people of Rome, their food and drink, and their problems about housing and drainage; there was liaison with the Lombard invaders as well as delicate negotiations with the imperial court. Gregory was himself beset moreover by 'frequent pains in the bowels and at every moment of the day exhausted by weakness of the internal organs and his breathing was affected by a low but unremitting fever'.[3] For Gregory, there was no dramatic suffering but what can be even more arduous, a pretty ordinary sense of never being really well; and in this for him the cross was applied personally and without remission. In the midst of his work Gregory found time for another labour, the conversion of the northern barbarians of the English race; he was, says Bede, 'our apostle, for he made our nation till then enslaved to idols into a church of Christ'.[4]

The defence of Rome, the conversion of the English, the war against the heretics and the constant spiritual warfare of prayer were not Gregory's only efforts at caring for the children of God. In the second book of the *Ecclesiastical History of the English People*, Bede wrote at length about Gregory, whom he revered not only as the apostle of the English but also as one of his own masters in commenting on the scriptures. He mentioned first Gregory's love of God and his desire for heaven, but he also described

2

a remarkable book called the *Pastoral Care* in which he set forth in the clearest manner what sort of persons should be chosen to rule the church and how these rulers ought to live, with how much discrimination they should instruct different types of listeners and how earnestly they ought each day to reflect on their own frailty.[5]

Pastoral Care[6] was a book forged by a monastic bishop in the midst of danger and distress, and it had immediate impact. Gregory sent his treatise to Leander, Bishop of Seville, in 591. The Emperor Maurice had it translated into Greek by Athanasius of Antioch. Carolingian councils recommended it; Hincmar of Rheims had it bound in with the canons and given to all bishops at their consecration, Bede recommended it, and Alfred the Great translated it. Gregory was a monk, but he was also a bishop, and it is this mixture which shows the way in which the central stillness of the monk was expressed in the care of the people of God in England. *Pastoral Care* is an immensely practical book, a handbook for bishops and also for anyone who has to care for others. In it there are no inspiring ideas about the survival of cultures or the education of the underprivileged. There is no dialogue with other religions, nor is it filled with instructions for crisis counselling. Gregory was concerned with the twofold love of God and neighbour among ordinary Christians, and it is as much about silence and stillness before God, where the pastor must always look to see his own faults and needs, as about the way in which the mercy he receives is to be given to others.

The first section is about the character proper for a candidate for the episcopate and the enormous responsibility involved: 'No art is taken in hand to be taught without having first been learned by earnest study.' The care of the people of God was for Gregory 'the very art of arts'. Himself a monk and lover of monks, he described himself in a way typical of monks: he was, he said, the weak one, the one most in need of mercy and the prayers of others, one who could hardly bear the distractions of the world and yet keep inner silence before God; the strong ones were not the monks of the cloister but those who could carry that stillness into the market-place. Therefore his instructions to those who had to care for others in such arduous and terrifying times begin and end with the pastors' care for themselves:

Let them consider how much they ought to be cleansed who carry living vessels in their bosom to the temple of eternity.

A pastor must declare the way of life to those that are under him by his words and by his example rather than by directions.

This programme of teaching by word and example became the great theme of the mission to the English. Gregory saw that, like the monk, the priest must know that he is chosen by God to govern only because he is the one who has received mercy, not because he is able, learned or noble. The pastor is not to be like rulers, overbusy with secular affairs, who are 'pleased if they are drowned in business'. The pastor's work is not his own; it is the work of Christ through him; the pastor should not want to be thought well of for what he does, for 'he is the friend of the bridegroom and must make sure that he is not loved in Christ's stead'. To make sure this is so, the pastor has an absolute obligation to make leisure for inward mysteries: 'secular business', Gregory says, 'must sometimes be endured out of compassion but never sought out with desire'.

Compassion and humility are the two basic aspects of the work of the pastor, the subject of the central sections of *Pastoral Care*:

Let the ruler be next to each one in compassion and soar above all in contemplation; let him learn from himself how to have mercy on others.

Such compassion was no soft or sentimental affair. Gregory insisted that if the pastor has been given the job of correction, then he must do it, though he added 'let him be a father by discipline but a mother by kindness; let them not feel sore through great harshness nor relaxed by too much softness'. Discretion, he says, is essential for a pastor; it is a nose, which can sniff out reality and truth; but he adds that the pastor must be careful that it is not a big nose, always poking itself into other people's affairs unasked; and, above all, that which should be kept secret should be respected and never made public out of vanity and curiosity.

This sense of discretion, of each person's dignity. appealed to the English, and in the Anglo-Saxon poem *The Wanderer* it is expressed vividly:

Often I have had to bemoan my anxieties at each dawning. There is now no living being to whom I dare plainly express my heart.[7]

This sense of the need for men to deal by themselves with difficulties is reflected in one of the sayings attributed to King Alfred: 'Do not tell your grief to a lesser man; tell it to your saddle-bow and ride forth singing.'

Each kind of person under the care of the pastor, Gregory says, has to be considered, not for the fearful things that have or have not happened to them but according to their nature and temperament and way of life. The pastor talks to married and unmarried differently, the sick differently from the healthy, old from young, rich from poor, those 'for whom all things turn out as they wish' differently from 'those for whom it is never so', and so on. There is a realism about *Pastoral Care* which takes into account both the fact of people as they are and the fact of the resurrection of Christ from the dead, and its chief concern is with the union of the two. Above all, the pastor must himself hurry towards the kingdom of God and make it his first task to ensure that others are able to do the same. He writes about the way a Christian cares for those for whom he is responsible before God, never losing sight of the pastor's own needs. In the midst of terrible events, Gregory did not resort to complaint against, or apology for, God; he did not try to find a new face to replace that of the Man of Sorrows: as another writer put it later, 'without form or comeliness, weak and nailed to a Cross, thus is truth known'.[8] Gregory simply got on with the work he had been given by God, putting into effect the deepest aspects of responsibility between Christians. The twofold love of God and man is neither to be discussed nor described but applied, because all the work done through the obedient man is the work of God. There is in his book an awareness that each person is someone in need and that the pastor is the servant of all because he himself most of all receives mercy upon his own need; and at the end he wrote:

> Being intent to show what a pastor ought to be, I, a foul painter, have portrayed a fair person; and I direct others to the shore of perfection while I am yet tossing on the waves of transgression.[9]

Pastoral Care was a formative book for the conversion of the English in giving advice about how the clergy should perform their tasks; the theme of preaching by word and example and the distinctively monastic tone of Gregory's work provided a basis for the English Church. Two centuries later, it provided a basis also for secular English government when King Alfred turned much of its advice into a handbook for secular as well as clerical rulers.

With such an 'apostle' as Gregory, the Christianity received by the Anglo-Saxons was essentially marked by compassion, patience and love. It was brought as a free gift, not enforced, and had careful regard for the people to whom it was offered. The spirituality of the English was shaped by the spirit of the Gregorian mission undertaken by monks sent into exile from their home for love of them. Already among the pagan Anglo-Saxons there were ideas and ideals that would be absorbed into the new Christian teaching: a longing for hope, love of journeys, a sense of community, of life in the kin-group, a fundamental love of one's lord as one's greatest friend, an instinct for splendour, and a feeling for the precariousness of life were all part of the Germanic world; Christianity gave this basis a wider view from the Church of the fathers, an understanding of suffering which is victory, a love of individuals which is tender, compassion for the poor, and a love of learning, linking the new converts with the early Church and the voice of the Gospel. It was the 'high king of heaven' who was the new Anglo-Saxon friend and lord. Gregory had initiated the mission to the Anglo-Saxons out of love and respect. In a famous story which reflects his approach to life as well as his love of wordplay, it was said that he saw English slaves for sale in Rome and admired their beauty:

> Alas that the author of darkness should have men so bright of face in his grip and that minds devoid of inward grace should bear so graceful an outward form. . . .

Calling them 'angels' rather than 'angles', seeing them taken away from the 'wrath of God' rather than from 'Deira', he called their king not 'Aella' but 'alleluia'[10] and immediately planned to go to Britain himself. Prevented from doing so because he became Pope, he nevertheless implemented his love of the slaves by sending Augustine and his companions. The arrival of Augustine in Kent set out the pattern Gregory had sent them to follow:

> Augustine and his companions came to meet King Aethelbert, endowed with divine not devilish power and bearing as their standard a silver cross and the image of our Lord and Saviour painted on a panel. They chanted litanies and uttered prayers to the Lord for their own eternal salvation and the

salvation of those for whom and to whom they had come. At the king's command they sat down and preached the word of life to himself and all his gesiths there present. Then he said to them 'The words and the promises you bring are fair enough, but because they are new to us and doubtful, I cannot consent to accept them and forsake those beliefs which I and the whole English race have held so long. But as you have come on a long pilgrimage and are anxious, I perceive, to share with us things which you believe to be true and good, we do not wish to do you harm; on the contrary, we will receive you hospitably and provide what is necessary for your support; nor do we forbid you to win all you can to your faith and religion by your preaching.' So he gave them a dwelling in the city of Canterbury, which was the chief city of kingdom. Though he rejoiced at their conversion and their faith, he compelled no one to accept Christianity.[11]

The alliance of the king and the missionaries which followed was to form a pattern for free co-operation between Church and state, and since the missionaries were also monks this established also the distinctively Anglo-Saxon situation of monastic bishops in their minsters. The respect with which the missionaries were treated and the long-drawn-out consultation between Aethelberht and his men were reflected later in the mission of his companion Paulinus to Northumbria, as was the presence of an educated and Christian queen, as a silent strength to the newcomers and a reassurance to their pagan husbands. The promise of salvation, a new kingdom, a wider life were all promises of hope, very much in line with the Anglo-Saxon understanding of the *gos-pel*, the Word of God, as good news, introducing them into new dimensions of life.

Augustine brought with him to the king a silver cross showing the glory of the cross along with a panel showing the human face of Jesus, and the monks immediately prayed, singing in procession, for mercy on themselves as well as those to whom they had come. Thus from the beginning vital Christian themes were presented in visual images to an unlettered culture. This combination of visual art with spoken word is another aspect of preaching by word and example; it is there in the great Anglo-Irish books such as Kells and Lindisfarne, and also in the presence of some more painted panels which were later brought from Rome and Gaul to England, confirming this first way of conveying truth:

He [Benedict Biscop] brought back many holy pictures of the saints to adorn the church of St Peter ... thus all who entered the church even those who could not read, whichever way they looked were able to contemplate the dear face of Christ and his saints even if only in a picture, and put themselves more firmly in mind of the Lord's incarnation and as they saw the decisive moment of the Last Judgement before their very eyes, be brought to examine their conscience with all due severity.[12]

Such paintings were not there for artistic effect; they were indeed examples of beauty but also an external replica of the truths being taught by words. Nor were they simply to be looked at and admired; they were to be applied in all the ways of self-knowledge and repentance that Gregory had so firmly taught.

When the missionaries had settled down in the Queen's church of St Martin in Canterbury, first of all they prayed, providing another 'example', another kind of picture, in their genuine and sincere example of Christian life which went alongside any preaching which they gave to those who asked for it:

They were constantly engaged in prayers, in fasts, in vigils, they preached the word of life to as many as they could; they despised all worldly things as foreign to them; they accepted only the necessaries of life from those whom they taught; in all things they practised what they preached and kept themselves prepared to endure adversities even to the point of dying for the truths they proclaimed.[13]

Gregory did not leave the missionaries to act alone. He wrote to them, in answer to any request for advice. The letters between Gregory and Augustine continued the themes of Gregorian spirituality in its new dress, with respect, with loving compassion, as well as with firmness and clarity. For example, in dealing with pagan places of worship Gregory wrote:

Things are not to be loved for the sake of a place but places are to be loved for the sake of good things; therefore choose from every individual church whatever things are devout, religious and right. And when you have collected these as it were into one bundle, see that the minds of the English grow accustomed to it.[14]

Later Gregory wrote in a similar vein to Bishop Mellitus, with a message for Augustine:

> Tell him what I have decided after long deliberation about the English people, namely that the temples of that race should by no means be destroyed but only the idols in them. . . . For if the shrines are well built it is essential that they should be changed from the worship of devils to the service of the true God . . . thus while outward rejoicings are preserved they will be able more easily to share in inward rejoicings.[15]

The letters between Gregory and Augustine shaped the spirituality not only of England but also of Europe; the English missionary Boniface asked for copies of them to use in his conversion of the Saxons on the continent and they remained an outstanding example of the way to convert non-believers, by love and prayer, by word and by example.

When Bede recorded the coming of Augustine and the mission of Paulinus, he wrote a long account of Gregory the Great; in it he recommended *Pastoral Care* as essential reading for the English; he also urged them to read the sermons preached by Gregory. He used many of these texts within his own commentaries on the Bible, which he offered as aids to establishing a true and lasting understanding of the Gospel among the English in his own day. The impact of the images and ideas of Gregory in these sermons can be illustrated by reference to the last paragraph of his sermon on the Ascension and his image of the seven leaps of Christ:

> And so the church says through Solomon: see how he comes leaping on the mountains, bounding over the hills. It pondered the height of his great work and said, see how he comes leaping upon the mountains. By coming for our redemption the Lord gave some leaps, if I may say so. Dearly beloved, do you want to recognise those leaps of his? From heaven to the womb, from the womb to the manger, from the manger to the cross, from the cross to the sepulchre; and from the sepulchre he returned to heaven. You see how truth, having made himself known in the flesh, gave some leaps for us to make us run after him. He exulted like a giant to run his course so that we might say to him from our hearts

'Draw me after you, let us run in the fragrance of your ointments'.[16]

This not only established a way of commenting on the Bible which lasted for many centuries, but the vividness of the imagery remained in the minds of the Anglo-Saxons as they created their own written language following the example of written Latin. They knew this passage through the preachers who had read Bede where he quoted this and the next paragraph of Gregory in his commentary on the *Song of Songs*.[17] In the Anglo-Saxon poem *Christ* the same theme was expanded with delight:

By grace of the Spirit, the glory of the servants of God emerged after the ascension of the eternal Lord. Concerning this, Solomon, son of David, a man most accomplished in poems, a ruler of nations, sang in spiritual enigmas and spoke these words: 'It shall be made known that the King of the angels, the Lord strong in his powers, will come springing upon the mountain, and leaping upon the high uplands; he will garland the hills and heights with his glory; he will redeem the world, all earth's inhabitants, by that glorious spring. The first leap was when he descended into a virgin, a maiden unblemished, and there assumed human form, free from sins, which came to be a comfort to all earth's inhabitants. The second spring was the birth of the Child when he was in the manger, wrapped up in garments in the form of a baby, the Majesty of all majesties. The third leap was the heavenly King's bound when he, the Father, the comforting Spirit, mounted upon the Cross. The fourth spring was into the tomb, secure in the sepulchre, when he quitted the tree. The fifth leap was when he humiliated the gang of hell's inhabitants in long torment and enchained the king within, the malignant mouthpiece of the fiends, in fiery fetters, where he still lies, fastened with shackles in prison, pinioned by his sins. The sixth leap was the Holy One's hope-giving move when he ascended to the heavens into his home of old. Then in that holy hour the throng of angels became enraptured with happy jubilation. They witnessed heaven's Majesty, the Sovereign of princes, reach his home, the gleaming mansions. The Prince's flittings to and fro became thereafter a perpetual delight to the blessed inhabitants of that city. Thus here on earth God's eternal Son sprang in leaps over the high hillsides, courageous across the mountains. So must we men

10

spring in leaps in the thoughts of our heart from strength to strength and strive after glorious things, so that we may ascend by holy works to the highest heaven where there is joy and bliss and the virtuous company of God's servants. It greatly behoves us that we should seek salvation with our heart.[18]

It is clear that the poetic and heroic traditions of Anglo-Saxon society were here merged with patristic imagery to produce new and vigorous Christian poetry.

The Anglo-Saxons did not understand the whole of the new message immediately; this absorbing of new values among old was a long-drawn-out process. But they built on a foundation firmly and consciously laid by Gregory the Great and the missionaries from the older Christian world of Rome and Gaul. It is remarkable how Gregory's personal sense of a need for God, his sense of sin and of the imminence of the Last Judgement which formed so large a part his own spirituality, found expression among those he had cared for. In an English prayer attributed to him in the tenth century there is his sense of the whole Church, of the Bible, of personal self-knowledge and humble but confident reliance on God, expressed through imagery proper to the new race:

> Almighty God, Lord and Ruler of All, Trinity,
> Father in the Son, Son in the Father, with the Holy Spirit,
> forever in all things, existing before all things,
> Lord blessed by all for ever:
> I commend my soul into your powerful hands,
> so that you may watch it
> by day and by night,
> at every moment and hour,
> Lord of the Angels, have mercy upon me.
> Guide me, King of the archangels,
> protect me through the prayers of the patriarchs,
> through the merits of the prophets,
> through the supplications of the apostles,
> through the victories of the martyrs,
> through the faith of the confessors,
> who have pleased you since the foundation of the world.
> Turn me, O Lord, from the desire for gluttony
> and give me the virtue of fasting.
> Drive far from me the spirit of fornication
> and give me the desire for chastity.

11

Take away from me greed
and make me willingly poor.
Restrain my anger
and inflame me with great sweetness
and love of God and of my neighbours.
Cut me off, O Lord, from the sadness of the world;
increase in me the joy of the Spirit.
Cast out from my mind, O Lord, the spirit of boasting,
and grant me the spirit of regret for wrong-doing.
Lessen my pride and imbue me with true humility.
I am unworthy and unhappy.
I was only freed from this sinful human body
by the grace of our Lord Jesus Christ.
I am a sinner and guilty of innumerable sins
and am not worthy to be called thy servant.
Awake in me the tears of repentance
and soften my hard and stony heart.
And light in me the fire of fear of you
because I am mortal ashes.
Free my soul from all besetting enemies
and keep me in your will
and teach me to do your commandments,
because you are my God.
To you be all honour and glory for ever and ever
Amen.[19]

Notes

1   Records of Romano-British Christianity are very scarce; some liter-
    ary sources have been preserved in Bede's *Ecclesiastical History of
    the English People*, ed. B. Colgrave and R. A. B. Mynors (Oxford,
    1969) (hereafter referred to as EHEP); there are materials relating
    to the lives of some saints, and there is the *Ruin of Britain* by Gildas;
    these are supplemented by the results of excavations. Place names
    and language studies suggest strongly the lack of contact between
    the earlier and the later Christians in Britain.

2   The earliest accounts of Gregory the Great are in EHEP, Book 2,
    and *The Earliest Life of Gregory the Great*, by an unknown 'monk of
    Whitby, ed. and trans. B. Colgrave (Kansas, 1968); a recent account
    is R. Markus, *Gregory the Great and His World* (Cambridge, 1997),
    with full bibliography.

3   Gregory often referred to his constant ill-health in his letters and in the Preface to his *Morals on the Book of Job*, where he saw himself as akin to Job, who was afflicted with boils.

4   EHEP, Book 2, cap. ii, p. 123.

5   Ibid., p. 127.

6   Gregory the Great, *Pastoral Care*, trans. Henry Davis SJ (New York, 1950).

7   *The Wanderer*, in *Anglo-Saxon Poetry*, trans. S. A. J. Bradley (London, 1982) (hereafter referred to as *Anglo-Saxon Poetry*), p. 332.

8   *The Meditations of Guigo 1*, trans. G. Mursell (Kalamazoo, 1995), p. 5.

9   *Pastoral Care*, Part IV, p. 237.

10 EHEP, Book 2, cap. i, p. 135.

11 Ibid., Book 1, xxv, p. 75.

12 Bede, *Lives of the Abbots of Wearmouth and Jarrow*, trans. D. H. Farmer, in *The Age of Bede* (Harmondsworth, 1965) (hereafter referred to as HA) cap. 6, pp. 190–1.

13 EHEP, Book 1, cap. xxvi, p. 77.

14 Ibid., cap. xxvii, p. 83.

15 Ibid., cap. xxx, p. 107.

16 Gregory the Great, *Forty Gospel Homilies*, trans, D. Hurst, (Cistercian Publications, Kalamazoo: 1990), Sermon 29, On the Ascension, p. 234.

17 Bede, *Commentary on the Song of Songs* (CCSL, 119B), p. 362.

18 *Christ 2*, in *Anglo-Saxon Poetry*, p. 225.

19 Prayer of St Gregory, from *The Book of Nunnaminster*, ed. Walter de Gray Birch (London, 1889) (hereafter referred to as *The Book of Nunnaminster*), pp. 58–60.

2

The Irish

'Christ in mouth of friend and stranger'

The main literary source for the history of the conversion of the English is Bede's *Ecclesiastical History of the English People*. There Bede told the story of a newly converted barbarian people, their history seen under the lens of the Gospel, as they became part of the Church which was living in the sixth and last age of the world.[1] In this work, Bede seems at first glance to be ruthlessly English and determinedly Roman. He was probably a Saxon himself, certainly a monk in a monastery founded in the Gaulish Roman pattern by the Saxon thane Benedict Biscop with the significant dedications of St Peter and St Paul, the great Roman apostles and martyrs. He was an admirer of the Latin doctors of the Church, especially Gregory the Great. But there is in Bede's life and works, and therefore also in the spirituality of his times, much that came to the island of England not directly from Rome but from Ireland. He was formed by and devoted to the Mediterranean Latin tradition of Christianity, but he saw it as being received from more than one source: from Rome through Gaul, certainly, but also from Rome through Ireland. In the first chapter of his account of the conversion of the English, he describes not one island but two:

> Ireland is broader than Britain, is healthier and has a much milder climate, so that snow rarely lasts there for more than three days. Hay is never cut in summer for winter use nor are stables built for their beasts. No reptile is found there nor

14

could a serpent survive.... In fact almost everything the island produces is efficacious against poison. The island abounds in milk and honey, nor does it lack vines, fish and birds. It is also noted for the hunting of stags and roedeer. It is properly the native land of the Irish ... they emigated from it ... and so formed the third nation in Britain.[2]

It sounds more like a description of the Islands of the Blessed, the imaginary lands of the West, than a factual description, but shows Bede's admiration of Ireland. Irish was also listed by Bede as one of the five languages of Britain which were all used for the sake of the Gospel,

all devoted to seeking out and setting forth one and the same kind of wisdom, namely the knowledge of sublime truth and true sublimity.[3]

The golden age of Northumbria in the seventh and eighth centuries, one of the most amazing flowerings of culture known, was based on a Northumbria filled with Irish and with Roman missionaries, and in other kingdoms the contacts between them were also both basic and pivotal. It is a false dichotomy to see English and Irish in opposition in these early centuries. The true picture is of a pagan culture, that of the Anglo-Saxons, in touch with Christian culure in two ways, namely from Rome through Gaul, and from Rome through Ireland. The attitude of Bede to the Irish in his own times, especially in what he had to say about Irish monks in England and in Ireland, can be seen as typical of his day; it is an area where there is so little information, especially about the Irish, that consideration of Bede's works here is vital.

There were clashes between the Roman missionaries and the British, that is to say, the Welsh, Christians. Augustine wrote to ask advice from Gregory about his relationship with them and received the reply:

we commit to you, my brother, all the bishops of Britain that the unlearned may be instructed, the weak strengthened by your counsel, and the perverse corrected by your authority.[4]

Augustine therefore invited the Welsh bishops to a conference, and urged them

that they should preserve catholic peace with him and undertake the joint labour of evangelizing the heathen for the Lord's sake.[5]

After a long dispute 'they were unwilling, in spite of the prayers, exhortations and rebukes of Augustine and his companions to give their assent', a stance which they maintained after a further long discussion, saying that 'they would not preach the way of life to the English nation'. The contacts between the Christians in Wales and the mission to the Anglo-Saxons seem to have ceased thereafter for that period. But with the Irish it was quite different, and any conflict over jurisdiction and the authority of Augustine did not flare up in his lifetime. In 664, over a hundred years after the coming of both Augustine and the Roman mission and Aidan and the Irish, a point of disagreement about the date at which Easter should be celebrated each year was seen to divide them; this was finally settled at the Council of Whitby, but it had in no way prevented joint evangelization earlier.

It is often supposed that there was an irreconcilable difference between Irish and Roman missionaries about the date of Easter, but it was in no way an anti-Irish, pro-Saxon tussle. Concern for the Easter dating was on a much wider and profounder scale than nationalism, as can be seen by remembering the people involved in the controversy itself. Nor was it a quarrel between different styles of Christianity, an institutional Roman and a free-spirited Celtic; both were concerned with the same problem and went about solving it in the same ways.

It was initially a practical problem. There was good reason for the different datings of Easter to come to a crisis in Northumbria in the mid-seventh century. On Easter Day 627, Edwin of Northumbria received baptism with his thanes and their followers at York from Paulinus, one of the companions of Augustine sent by Pope Gregory from Rome; it was 12 April 627, a date for Easter calculated according to the Roman method. In 633, six years later, Edwin was killed in battle at Hatfield Chase and Paulinus fled with the Queen to Kent. James the Deacon remained behind near Catterick, and when peace was restored a year later James (who was later present at the Council of Whitby) 'instructed many in singing after the manner of Rome and the Kentish people'.[6] After a year, there was bitter warfare between the pagan invaders and the new Christian claimant to the throne, Oswald, who had been in exile and received Christian baptism from Irish monks on Iona. He became king in Northumbria and at once introduced missionaries from Iona, who followed the Irish customs. In one year, and with Roman Christians still alive and active, the Roman calculation for the date of Easter was surely still assumed to be correct in Northumbria. The difference came with the new missionaries, friends of the king, who knew his Christianity first from the Irish, who kept Easter on a different day from the Roman missionaries, and indeed from the rest of the Church. The second stage in the conversion of Northumbria, therefore, accidentally differed from the first in this one matter. Paulinus, Edwin, Ethelburgh and their daughter Eanflaed, the wife of Oswiu, naturally calculated according to the modern Roman revised dating; Aidan and Oswald and Oswiu equally naturally according to the unrevised dating which had also originally come from Rome. An unconscious difference, but confusing for the Northumbrians.

For the first Anglo-Saxon Christians, Easter was the central point of the year, the moment when by baptism they entered into the new life in Christ about which they had heard from the missionaries sent from Rome and from Ireland. It was not to them an arbitrary date but the pivot of the whole of the cosmos, the central moment when reality was revealed in the face of Jesus Christ. Here evangelical doctrine, corporate liturgy and inner devotion were united, and in this unity they discovered also their oneness with the Church in other times and places. That the missionaries who preached the Gospel to them should differ about the date on which this Paschal mystery should be celebrated was both confusing and scandalous; where external practice was not something separate from internal faith, the implications of such division were in no way trivial.

The Anglo-Saxons were enthusiastic about Easter. With the advice of Gregory to Augustine to support them, they did not find the idea of a festival in spring entirely new; they saw a connection between the date of Easter and their custom of celebrating a spring goddess; in his book on natural science, Bede refers to the Anglo-Saxon name for the feast of the Resurrection:

> Easter-month, which is now called the paschal month, was formerly so called from a goddess of theirs [the English] called Eostre and since her festival was celebrated then it had that name. By that name they now call the time of pascha, customary observance giving its name to a new solemnity.[7]

The name remained pagan, as indeed did the word 'Lent' (spring) which was used rather than the Latin *jejunium* (the fast), and so did the days of the week, but in each case the content was radically different. Bede added 'I thank you, good Jesu, for turning us from such vanities, and allowing us to offer the sacrifice of praise'.

Again and again in Bede's commentaries on the Scriptures, which he sent to priests throughout England to help them in their preaching, the centrality of the resurrection of Christ was discussed, not only in his commentaries on the Gospels but also in his work on the Old Testament. In his history of the English nation as a race new-born into Christ, Bede placed at the centre a chapter which gives an account of the discussion at the Council of Whitby in 664 of the differing dates at which Easter was celebrated by the Christians of the new Roman and the old Roman–Irish traditions. In Book 5, he also quoted at length a letter to Nectan, King of the Picts, which originated with his master Ceolfrith, about the correct way to calculate the date. As an astronomer, as a historian and as a Christian, Bede was deeply concerned by the accounts he read of the differences among Christians of this island, which were resolved just before his own lifetime, about this sacred moment in the calendar. It was a matter which interested him as an astronomer, since the date depends upon the accurate calculation of the cycles of the years, by the moon and by the sun, and their alignment. Bede was well able to calculate the correct evolution of the years and was aware of the most up-to-date tables available for doing so, to which he himself contributed. As a historian, he had read in the church history of Eusebius of the grave view taken by the early Church about differences in the observance of this date. He had read the fierce words of the Fathers on the subject and knew of the anathemas which had accompanied its resolution at the Council of Nicaea. He was also aware of the unease of mind caused by the practical difficulties of difference which had disedified Anglo-Saxon Christians in Northumbria before Whitby:

> Queen Eanflaed and her people ... observed [Easter] as she had seen it done in Kent. ... Hence it is said that in these days it sometimes happened that Easter was celebrated twice in the same year, so that the king had finished the fast and was keeping Easter Sunday, while the queen and her people were still in Lent and observing Palm Sunday.[8]

But more than this, the matter of a united date for the observance of Easter had to do with theology: such a division brought disunity into the heart and centre of the Christian religion, and to differ in practice was inseparable from exhibiting error in doctrine.

Where those who differed did so in ignorance while their conduct and prayer remained sound, Bede himself did not approve of their digression, but because the central mystery of faith was his first concern, he did not deal out condemnation. He wrote, for instance, of Aidan, his ideal among monks:

All these things I greatly admire and love in this bishop ... I neither praise nor approve of him insofar as he did not observe Easter at the proper time ... I do approve of this, that in his celebration of Easter he had no other thought in his heart, he reverenced and preached no other doctrine than we do, namely the redemption of the human race by the passion, resurrection and ascension into heaven of the one mediator between God and men, even the man Jesus Christ.[9]

Easter, the moment of attention to the passion and resurrection of Christ, was not just a feast on its own that could be celebrated at whim. On it hung the whole of the Christian year, with Lent and Pentecost around it. It was also, as for Edwin of Northumbria, one of the rare moments for the entry of new members into the Church by baptism in which they personally, after instruction, put on the living and dying of the Lord Jesus. Nor was the date of the death and resurrection of Jesus arbitrary: it was a historical fact in time, and because of it all time was changed into a new configuration. Tradition had linked the date into the ebb and flow of the universe, of all creation, and it is not surprising to find that one of Bede's most intense passages on the calculation of Easter occurs in his commentary on the account of the creation of the world in Genesis. In his first book on the calculation of time, he linked the calculation of the date of Easter with the created world in detail: the pasch, he says, is celebrated

when the equinox is passed, that the shadow of death may be vanquished by the true light ... in the first month of the year, which is called the month of New Fruits, so that the joy of a new life may be celebrated ... at the turn of the moon, to show how the glory of the mind is turned from earthly things to heavenly ones ... on the Lord's Day, when the light shows the triumph of Christ and our own resurrection.[10]

In the letter to Nectan he added:

We are commanded to keep the full moon of the paschal month after the vernal equinox, the object being that the sun should first make the day longer than the night and then the moon can show to the world her full orb of light because the 'Sun of righteousness with healing in his wings' (Mal 4:2), that is, the Lord Jesus, overcame all the darkness of death by the triumph of his resurrection.[11]

There was nothing there that any Irishman would object to. Why some of the Irish and also some of the English differed from the new Roman missionaries about this crucial date was not a matter of alternative symbolism or theology or biblical study, but of calendric calculation. It was not, as Wilfrid suggested at Whitby, because they were Quartodecimans, that is, those who kept the feast of Easter on any day of the week provided it was the fourteenth of Nisan. The Irish calculated Easter in a perfectly orthodox manner; the problem was that they were using lunar tables which had reached them from Rome and were made by Victorius of Aquitaine on a 95-year cycle, and were less accurate than those which had replaced them, that is, those of Dionysius the Small. In 525 he had produced a table for calculating Easter based on a lunar cycle of 532 years, that is, 28 periods of nineteen years each, reckoned from the year of the birth of Christ.[12] Other minor differences also caused the dates sometimes to coincide, sometimes to be a week apart, sometimes four weeks apart. To Anglo-Saxon Christians such differences were intolerable and after 664 they, and most of the Irish, agreed to observe the new Roman Easter; by 731, even the conservative Iona had followed suit.

That was the point of discussion at Whitby. When we look at who said what and why, it was all more mixed-up than at first appears. It was not a matter of the arrogant men from Rome baring their teeth at the simple Irish at all. At the Council of Whitby, who supported which side? There was no clear-cut division in terms of nationalism. An epitome of the mingling of traditions is seen in Hilda, the hostess on this occasion.[13] Hilda was an Anglo-Saxon princess (614–680), younger daughter of Hereric, nephew of Edwin of Northumbria, and of Breguswith; she was born while her father was a prisoner of the British in Elmet, who later killed him by poison. Her mother, before her birth, feeling a sense of great loss, dreamt that she found 'a most precious necklace under her garment . . . such a blaze of light that it filled all Britain with its grace and splendour'. Hilda was brought up at the court of the Saxon Edwin. One sister, Hereswith (names of both parents), married the Saxon king of East Anglia, and then became a nun at the convent of Chelles in Gaul. Hilda was baptized with Edwin and his court on 12 April 627, aged thirteen, in the new church dedicated to St Peter in York by Paulinus. Perhaps she was part of the group of nobles who fled south when Edwin was killed by Aethelred. She was thus by birth one of the Saxon invaders, and her first experience of Christianity was of that brought by the Roman missionaries. In 647, twenty years later when she was 33, Hilda decided to be a nun and went to her nephew in East Anglia for a year, planning to go to join her sister in the Gaulish convent at Chelles. But she came to know and revere the missionary from Iona, Aidan, and he persuaded her to stay in England, first as part of a new group at Hartlepool. Then, when the abbess Heiu left for a life of greater seclusion, Hilda became abbess. She was given charge of Aelfflaed, one-year-old daughter of King Oswiu of Northumbria, after his success at the battle of the Winwead. Two years later Oswiu gave her more land at Whitby, where she ruled a new monastery. She was greatly revered and loved: 'All who knew her called her mother.' She made the royal monastery of Whitby, the place of the burial of the rulers of Northumbria, a place of serious Christian education, where she trained five bishops including the saintly John of Beverley. There also the first English poet, Caedmon, became a monk and there the earliest *Life of Pope Gregory the Great* was written. Hilda was hostess to the Council of Whitby where, under the influence of Aidan and Colman, she inclined at first towards the Irish side. Possibly there was a personal antagonism between her and Wilfrid since she later accused Wilfrid to Rome in the last year of her life. Hilda died in 680, the year in which Bede entered Wearmouth. In her life there is a mixture of Anglo-Saxon, Roman and Irish elements which blended together imperceptibly.

No clear line can be drawn about others, either: Cedd of the East Saxons had been consecrated by the Irish but acted as a careful and impartial interpreter at Whitby; King Oswiu, who called the council, had been baptized by the Irish and spoke Irish but accepted in the end without hesitation the new Roman calculation. Wilfrid himself, the architect of the Roman arguments and the first Englishman to appeal to Rome, had been educated in the Irish monastery of Lindisfarne. Agilbert, who ordained Wilfrid priest, though born in Gaul had been educated in Ireland. Prince Aldfrith, who was a friend of Wilfrid, gave him the abbey of Ripon, but only after offering it to Cuthbert and Eata of

Melrose, 'who followed the Irish ways'. The same Prince Aldfrith, son of a Saxon king, was a learned man, educated in Ireland, who exchanged land with Benedict Biscop in order to have a book of cosmology. A later prince of the same sternly English name was exiled to Ireland and came to the throne of Northumbria in 685 on the death of his half-brother Ecgfrith. He was a pupil of Aldhelm, the great English teacher and scholar at Malmesbury. His mother was a direct descendant of Irish high kings and the Irish annals record his death as that of an Irish poet called Flan Fina.

So almost everyone at Whitby had close and friendly contact with both Roman and Irish missionaries; it was not a clash of opposites, but an argument between friends on a matter the importance of which united them far more than the details divided. There was no sense that Romans were good and Irish were bad. In this matter of the Easter date, what needed sorting out were errors of calculation, whoever did it. And likewise with conduct: no one was to be judged as Roman, English or Irish: such divisions were not appropriate. Roman missionaries, Saxons and Irish were praised for some things, but not admired for others, in their conduct as Christians. For instance, Irish missionaries were praised for many apostolic virtues, but there were facets of the Irish character that were not seen as admirable, even when linked to evangelical zeal. The Irish were fervent preachers but their readiness to correct others was not always an advantage. Perhaps in the lands of the Irish, where there had been Christians since the days of Patrick, what was most needed was challenge and fierceness. But the English were not yet Christian; they 'needed the milk of the word'. So when a fierce hell-fire preacher was sent to Northumbria from Iona, he was sent home again and replaced by the wiser Aidan.[14] The Irish temper was not even very efficacious in discussions among the Irish themselves: when Ronan, an Irishman who had been in Gaul and accepted the new calculations for Easter, argued on the subject with his compatriot, Finan,'who was a man of fierce temper', he enraged him instead of convincing him by the way in which he disputed with him.[15] The worldly life of the nuns at Coldingham was rebuked by the Irishman Adamnan, who saw fire descending on their monastery, even though they had begun under the care of the Saxon queen-abbess Aebba, a friend of Cuthbert.[16] After the Council of Whitby, Colman, who at that moment refused to accept the decision about Easter, left Northumbria with some Irish disciples and 30 English monks who shared his opinions. They eventually settled on the island of Inishbofin, off the coast of Galway. Problems arose, not about doctrine but about conduct:

> The Irish, in summer time when the harvest had to be gathered, left the monastery and wandered about ... then when winter came they returned and expected to have a share in the things which the English had provided.[17]

The difference caused the English to leave the Irish on the island while they founded a new monastery at Mayo on the mainland. The freedom of the Irish formed a contrast with the organized English, the basis of much later English–Irish humour.

What, then, did the Irish contribute to the evangelical grounding of the Anglo-Saxon converts? The generosity with which they came to preach to the Anglo-Saxons was contrasted with the care with which the Welsh kept themselves to themselves, not with the Roman-based missionaries who had come with equal generosity and further from home. They came like the Romans without a political agenda, and their ways were fundamentally similar. In both cases, these missionaries were monks and came from an established background in Christianity. As the different cultures came to a new field of mission, their own ways were inevitably changed by the culture and expectations of their converts; and in this emerging Christianity both Irish and Romano–Gaulic were transformed into a new tradition which could be called English.

It is therefore not easy to see what was distinctive about the Irish contribution. Nevertheless some points can be made. First: the Irish were known for their Latin learning in the Scriptures. Bede himself was taught by the Irish scholar Trumhere. The Saxon monk Egbert went among the Irish, learned what he could there, and returned to preach in England. Scripture study, and the Latin which made it possible, were however, sought in both England and Ireland after a while, especially when the Greek scholar Theodore had established his outstanding school at Canterbury.[18] Aldhelm, a contemporary of Bede,[19] also taught with authority at Malmesbury. Aldhelm at Malmesbury urged the prior advantage of study in England and himself experimented with 'Famina Hisperica', a late Latin style originating from Aquitaine in the fifth century, with a specialized and fantastic vocabulary and style. Aldhelm seems to have been like the hermit with his cat, Pangur Ban:

Hunting mice is his delight,
hunting words I sit all night.

The Anglo-Saxon love of wordplay was enhanced by the new craft of writing which both groups of missionaries brought. They learned to write in Latin but at once their enthusiasm for writing extended to inventing a written form for their own langage, composing in it riddles and epigrams which were inherent in their oral culture, but also religious poems usually based on the Bible. The Irish and the Roman texts contributed to the new forms. In insular manuscript illumination, a strong influence came with the books brought from the Mediterranean world, but also through those from Ireland. Whatever is thought about the exact place of writing of some manuscripts, the extraordinary unity of the insular hand is certain. Lindisfarne, Kells, Durrow, etc. show a unity of culture, with subtle and sophisticated visual images as well as fine workmanship.[20]

Secondly, the Irish were praised for their evangelical holiness: they preached and lived in the pattern of the apostles, with an instinctive concern for the poor. Established as Christians and with the quick, evangelical zeal of their race, they were particularly keen to convey their understanding of the centrality of salvation for each person regardless of rank. They belonged to a close-knit clan culture where the bishop was one of the tribe, but with special powers of rebuke at his disposal. They had the courage to challenge anyone, even kings, and to make a vivid dramatic gesture which would call for more response than careful sermons. For instance:

He [King Oswiu] had given Bishop Aidan an excellent horse so that, though he was normally accustomed to walk, he could ride if he had to cross a river or if any other urgent necessity compelled him. A short time afterwards Aidan was met by a beggar who asked him for an alms. He at once alighted and offered the horse with all its royal trappings to the beggar; for he was extremely compassionate, a friend of the poor and a real father to the wretched. The king was told of this and, happening to meet the bishop as they were going to dinner, he said, 'My lord bishop, why did you want to give a beggar the royal horse intended for you? Have we not many less valuable horses or other things which would have been good enough to give to the poor, without letting the beggar have the horse which I had specially chosen for your own use?'

24

The bishop at once replied, 'O King, what are you saying? Surely this son of a mare is not dearer to you than that son of God?' After these words they went in to dine. The bishop sat down in his own place and the king, who had just come in from hunting, stood warming himself by the fire with his thegns. Suddenly he remembered the bishop's words; at once he took off his sword, gave it to a thegn, and then hastening to where the bishop sat, threw himself at his feet and asked his pardon. 'Never from henceforth', he said, 'will I speak of this again nor will I form any opinion as to what money of mine or how much of it you should give to the sons of God.'[21]

The Anglo-Saxon concept of the king as the giver of gifts, whose presents were designed to show the generosity and wealth of the king himself, was challenged by the ideal of despising riches and giving to the poor, of the value of man as being made in the image of God. This was a contrast not with Roman missionaries, but with Germanic culture. The missionaries from Rome could equally act out a rebuke to kings: when Eadbald, the son of Aethelberht, reverted to paganism in Kent on the death of his father, and the three pagan sons of Saeberht of the East Saxons did the same, Bishop Laurence was ready to flee in despair. However, he dreamed

> that St Peter scourged him hard and long and reminded him that 'I suffered death, even the death of the cross ... that I might be crowned with him'.[22]

The reminder of the centrality of the Cross of Christ in relation to suffering and the duty of the Christian to be ready, as the missionaries had said at first, 'to die if need be', convinced Laurence to remain; but he did not treat the dream as a private and personal reminder only; he went to the King as soon as morning had come, drew back his robe and showed him the marks of his stripes:

> When he heard that it was for the sake of his salvation that the bishop had suffered such torments and wounds at the hands of the apostle of Christ, he was greatly afraid ... accepted the Christian faith and was baptized.[23]

In both cases, the bishops were present at the courts of kings, with ready access to them; both used their understanding of the

Scriptures to correct and explain the new gospel in its relation not only to belief but also to conduct.

Third, both Irish and Anglo-Saxons were part of kin-groups and the first missionaries from Rome understood this insofar as they became bishops of peoples rather than places, the people of Kent, the people of Northumbria, of Lindisfarne, etc. It was later that the bishops became territorial, with bishops of Canterbury, London, York etc. But the Irish also conveyed to the Anglo-Saxons their monastic understanding of the value of each person, a concern with the heart, with the motive, which was also reflected in the Irish Penitential Codes of the seventh century; there a tariff was set out for penance for sins, but with the comment:

> This is carefully to be considered in all penance: the length of time anyone remains in his faults; with what learning he is instructed; with what passion he is assailed; with what courage he stands; with what tearfulness he is seen to be afflicted.[24]

Here was a concern with the inner motivation of sinners which belonged to the monastic concept of the spiritual father, found in the world of early monasticism and conveyed to the west in the works of John Cassian. The care for the individual was not, of course, exclusively Irish; the approach of Gregory the Great, as has been seen, was the same, but the idea of official penance done publicly for grave sin had predominated in the early Church, and it was with the combination of the Irish and Gregorian idea of care for the soul, by advice and counsel, treating sin as a sickness to be cured as well as a wickedness to be punished, that the idea of confession and forgiveness developed. When Theodore, the Greek who was the seventh Archbishop of Canterbury, composed his Penitential, it was this ideal of penance as a remedy for the soul that predominated.

With regard to dreams, visions and supernatural experiences, the Saxons received a great deal from the Irish as well as from the written traditions of the early Church. The sense of the presence of the angels which filled the *Life of St Columba*[25] was popular, as was the account of a visit to heaven and hell by the Irish monk Fursey;[26] so much so that the Northumbrian married man Drythelm was eagerly heard when he recounted his own journeys into these other worlds.[27] Moreover, though the pagan past of early Christianity was six centuries distant for the missionaries from the Mediterranean world, for the Irish as much as for the Saxons it was more recent. For them both the menace of demons was real and their need of protection great. The well-known hymn attributed to St Patrick combined both the terror of temptation and sin, the dominance of magic, with the strength of dependence on Christ's indwelling and is one of the greatest examples of Irish devotional expression from this period. It embodies the richness of the Irish contribution to the rapidly emerging English spirituality. There the terror of demons, the sense of a pagan background of menace, is balanced by the strength of reliance on the basic doctrines and events of the life of Christ and the even stronger sense of his indwelling as the Trinity in every aspect of new life for the individual, which is seen as freedom, liberation from the limiting and dehumanizing pagan world:

> I bind unto myself today
> The strong name of the Trinity,
> By invocation of the same,
> The Three in One, the One in Three ...
> I bind unto myself today
> The power of God to hold and lead,
> His eye to watch, His might to stay,
> His ear to hearken to my need ...
> The wisdom of my God to teach,
> His hand to guide, His shield to ward,
> The word of God to give me speech,
> His heavenly host to be my guard ...
> Against all Satan's spells and wiles,
> Against false words of heresy,
> Against the knowledge that defiles,
> Against the heart's idolatry,
> Against the wizard's evil craft,
> Against the death wound and the burning,
> The choking wave, the poisoned shaft,
> Protect me, Christ, till Thy returning ...
> Christ be with me, Christ within me
> Christ behind me, Christ before me
> Christ beside me, Christ to win me
> Christ to comfort and restore me.
> Christ beneath me, Christ above me
> Christ in quiet, Christ in danger
> Christ in hearts of all that love me,
> Christ in mouth of friend and stranger.[28]

Notes

1   Bede, *De Temporibus*, cap. xvi.

2   EHEP, Book 1, cap. i, pp. 19–21.

3   Ibid., p. 17.

4   Ibid., Book 1, cap. xxvii, pp. 81–3.

5   Ibid., Book 2, cap. ii, p. 135.

6   Ibid., Book 2, cap. xx, p. 207.

7   Bede, *De Temporum Ratione*, cap. xv, pp. 178–9, ed. C. W. Jones, CCSL 123B.

8   EHEP, Book 3, cap. xxv, p. 297.

9   Ibid., Book 3, cap. xvii, p. 267.

10 Bede, *De Temporum Ratione*, cap. lxiiii; p. 456.

11 EHEP, Book 5, cap. xxi, p. 543.

12 Cf. C. W. Jones, *Opera de Temporibus* (Cambridge, MA, 1943).

13 EHEP, Book 4, cap. xxiii, pp. 405–15.

14 Ibid., Book 3, cap. v, p. 229.

15 Ibid., Book 3, cap. xxv, p. 297.

16 Ibid., Book 4, cap. xxv, pp. 421–7.

17 Ibid., Book 4, cap. iv, p. 347.

18 Cf. EHEP, Book 4, caps i & ii, pp. 329–37; for Theodore's work on biblical commentary cf. *Biblical Commentaries from the Canterbury School of Theodore and Hadrian*, ed. B. Bischoff and M. Lapidge (Cambridge, 1994).

19 Cf. Aldhelm, *The Prose Works*, trans. M. Lapidge and M. Herren (London, 1979).

20 Cf. George Henderson, *From Durrow to Kells: The Insular Gospel Books 650–800* (London, 1987).

21 EHEP, Book 3, cap. xiv, p. 259.

22 Ibid., Book 2, cap. vi, p. 155.

23 Ibid.

24 'The Penitential of Cummean' in *The Irish Penitentials*, ed. L. Bieler (Dublin, 1975), p. 133.

25 Cf. Adomnan, *Life of Columba*, ed. and trans. A. O. Anderson and M. O. Anderson (London, 1961); also a translation with informative introduction by R. Sharpe (Harmondsworth, 1981).

26 EHEP, Book 3, cap. xix, pp. 269–77.

27 Ibid., Book 5, cap. xii, 489–99.

28 'The Loric of St Patrick', trans. F. Alexander, *Hymns Ancient and Modern* (London, 1924), no. 655, pp. 565–70.

3

Prayer together

'We draw near to heavenly mysteries'

The Anglo-Saxons received the message of Christianity from the world of the early Church through Roman Gaul and through Ireland. The central ingredient in their new life was that contact with God which is called prayer. Prayer among the Anglo-Saxons was done together in church and also in private. But without a skeleton a body cannot do anything and prayer in church provided that essential framework on which all personal prayer and conduct could be based. The pattern of gathering together in church for worship was a gift brought by both Augustine and Aidan:

> [in the church of St Martin] they [Augustine and his companions] first began to meet to chant the psalms, to pray, to say mass to preach and to baptise ... until they received greater liberty to build or restore churches.[1]

> When Aidan arrived, king Oswald gave him the island of Lindisfarne for his monastic centre and ... many came [to Northumbria] preaching the word with great devotion.... Churches were built in various places and people flocked together with joy to hear the word.[2]

The churches were themselves images of the glory of the kingdom of heaven and the barbaric love of gold, of light and colour, was reflected in the new stone buildings which arose at Canterbury, York, Ripon, Hexham, Wearmouth and Jarrow and, eventually, Lindisfarne. The wonder of the fact of God in Christ redeeming the world to himself was conveyed in words by preaching but even more by the beauty of holiness in the ceremonies and in the form and decoration of the churches themselves. In the year 674, King Ecgfrith of Northumbria received a visit from Benedict Baducing, now called Biscop, former thane of his predecessor King Oswiu; he had travelled widely and now returned home carrying books and relics and wanting to found a monastery. The king gave him land at the mouth of the Wear where he founded a monastery dedicated to St Peter. Details were recorded about the new buildings at Monkwearmouth:

> when the building was nearing completion he sent his agents across to France to bring over glaziers — craftsmen as yet unknown in Britain — to glaze the windows in the body of the church and in the chapels and in the clerestory. He was also a dedicated collector of everything necessary for the service of church and altar and saw to it that what could not be obtained at home was shipped over from abroad.[3]

Already a second monastery had been founded when, six years previously, the king had given more land for the building of St Paul's at Jarrow. The learned and experienced Ceolfrith had gone there with seventeen monks from St Peter's, Monkwearmouth. The second house was built on the understanding that

> the two houses should be bound together by the one spirit of peace and harmony and united by continuous friendship and goodwill ... neither was anyone to attempt to disturb the brotherly love that would unite the two houses just as it had bound together the two chief apostles, Peter and Paul.[4]

The house at Jarrow was founded in brotherly love but also in great suffering. Bede joined the house under the special care of Ceolfrith a year after its foundation and in 685, having seen its construction, he was present at its dedication; an inscription was placed there which still exists, mentioning Ecgfrith the patron as well as Ceolfrith the abbot:

> The dedication of the basilica of St Paul on the ninth day before the Kalens of May in the fifteenth year of King Ecgfrith and the fourth year of Ceolfrith the abbot and with God's help, the founder of this church.[5]

But in the same year Ecgfrith was killed at Nechtansmere in his unjust battle against the Picts, and of all the eager young men who were monks at Jarrow only the abbot and Bede remained after an onslaught of a fatal disease referred to as 'plague'.[6]

Ceolfrith continued Benedict Biscop's policy of building and beautifying the churches of the monasteries. They built in stone, not only out of a desire to emulate the great buildings of Rome, but from a sense of the future: stone would last and when all the men had gone the stones would pray. Stability and continuity were the concern of the abbots, causing them to make settlements with kings and popes, as well as securing beautiful altar vessels and vestments and paintings worthy of the house of God. Inner building of the mind was also helped when Ceolfrith 'doubled the number of books in the libraries of both monasteries'. Like Abbot Eanfrith at Lindisfarne later, he 'found the church wood and left it stone'.

Bede saw the building of the stone churches with wondering eyes, and what he observed was reflected in his later writings:

so when we in our humility have some task to perform, for example when we are building a house, we begin the work by preparing our material and after this beginning we dig deeply. Next we put stones into this foundation and then we place walls upon it in rising courses of stones and so little by little we reach completion in accomplishing the task on which we have set out.

Perhaps they used bricks instead of stones and bitumen instead of cement because those districts lacked a sufficient quantity of stones for the completion of so great a work or because they knew that a wall built of brick offered greater resistance to the danger of fires. Bitumen is made from trees: it is also made from earth or water.[7]

But he also wrote with a perception about buildings that went beyond the surface. He used the simile of building often in discussion of the life of the soul:

The house of God which king Solomon built in Jerusalem was made a figure of the holy universal church which from the first of the elect to the last to be at the end of the world is daily being built through the grace of the king of peace namely its redeemer. It is still partly in a state of pilgrimage from him on earth and partly having escaped from the hardships of its sojourn already reigns with him in heaven where when the last judgement is over it is to reign com-

pletely with him. To this house belong the chosen angels ...
the terrestrial temple was a figure of us all ... in some
respects it describes the unclouded happiness of the angels in
heaven, in others the invincible patience of mankind on earth,
in others the help of the angels bestowed on mankind and in
others again it will show the struggles of mankind rewarded
by the angels.[8]

The building of a church was hard labour both physically and
spiritually, and there were those stones which found no place
there. Bede describes the deaths of an unabsolved thane and a
unrepentant monastic blacksmith as examples of the stones which
were broken by the harsh and demanding process:

Cement is made from stones which have been burnt and
turned to ash. These stones which were previously strong and
firm, each one by itself, are worked upon by the fire in such
a way that when they have been softened by the addition of
heat and when they have been joined together in a better
way, they are themselves able to bind other stones which
have been placed in position in a wall. Thus they soon receive
again in a better way the strength that for a little while they
seemed to have lost.[9]

The stones were not required to be perfect but to be malleable.
The Roman stones from older walls were used, but cut and shaped
and put into place among the rest. Christianity was not about a
man alone with the alone but about a community, a church, a
building, which had its foundations in heaven.

These lovely monasteries, built by zeal and love, were much
more significant than simply a place the monks called home. In
Bede's sermon about Benedict Biscop, but elsewhere again and
again, he used the image of building in stones as the image of
building men into the church of Christ. In his treatises *On the
Temple* and *On the Tabernacle*, *On Esdras and Nehemiah*, and
above all in his sermons for the anniversary of the dedication of
the church at Jarrow, the significance of the buildings was brought
out, along with a delight in their beauty. Two sermons on the
dedication of St Paul's were most probably preached on 23 April
between the years 703 and his death in 735; this can be narrowed
a little further since he was ill for a year before his death:

We ... spend the night in vigil joyfully singing additional
psalms and hearing a larger number of lessons in a church

where many lights are burning and the walls are adorned more lavishly than usual.[10]

Having set the scene of the night vigil, with the illumination and decoration around the walls, he continued in a deeper vein:

My brothers, let us love wholeheartedly the beauty of the eternal house we have from God in the heavens and let us take care to think attentively about the place of the tabernacle of his glory and prompt one another to do likewise. Above all let us ask one thing from him and let us seek this with unwearied attention that we may be worthy to dwell in his house all the days of our life, that is, to be filled with the bliss of everlasting life and light. He does not reject or scorn the prayer of the poor when we entreat him for what he himself loves, but he graciously hearkens and he will grant us to see his good things in the land of the living, Jesus Christ our Lord, who lives and reigns with the Father in the unity of the Holy Spirit, God throughout all ages of ages. Amen.[11]

In a sermon preached for the same anniversary in another year, he stressed the building that should be done by good works:

We must not suppose that only the building in which we come together to pray and celebrate the mysteries is the Lord's temple and that we ourselves who come together in the Lord's name are not more fully his temple . . . let us avoid winter's image lest the Lord on coming into our hearts find them numb from lack of charity's ardour. Although the labours of this age are burdensome and prolonged whatever ends in eternal blessedness seems shortlived and trifling. . . . Let us busy ourselves with the mutual help of charity so that finding all of us with cheerful hearts and tireless in good works, which he has commanded us to do, Jesus Christ our Lord may bring us all to the reward of the perpetual vision of him which he has promised.[12]

What was the content of the worship offered inside these churches? For the monks — and each group of clergy with their bishop consisted predominantly of monks — the Offices were said or sung together during the day and night; the chief element in such recitation was the psalter. The psalms were used in public corporate worship from the earliest times, those psalms which were appropriate being selected for prayer at the beginning and ending of the day. John Chrysostom, bishop and focal point of the liturgical life of the Church in fourth-century Constantinople, recommended the psalms for all times and occasions in a lively sermon, with a refrain of 'first, last and central is David':

> If we keep vigil in the church, David comes first, last and central. If early in the morning we chant songs and hymns, first, last and central is David again. If we are occupied with the funeral solemnities of those who have fallen asleep, David is first, last and central.

Not only in the solemn liturgies of the great church, he says, but in all gatherings of Christians, learned or not, the psalter is central:

> O amazing wonder! many who have made little progress in literature know the psalter by heart. Nor is it only in cities and churches that David is famous, in the village market, in the desert, in uninhabitable land or if girls sit at home and spin, he excites the praises of God.

Clearly, he is talking about all the holy people of God in their ordinary ways of life, not the specialist group of monks, for he then goes on to mention them:

> In monasteries, among those holy choirs of angelic armies, David is first, last and central. In convents of virgins, where are the communities of those who imitate Mary, in deserts where there are men crucified to the world, who live their life in heaven with God, David is first, last and central. All other men at night are asleep, David alone is active, and gathering the saints of God into seraphic bands, he turns earth into heaven and converts men into angels.[13]

The psalms were uniquely prized by the whole Church; and like all Scripture, they were seen as more than human words, for in them God spoke through David as a prophet of Christ. In various ways the liturgy indicated to believers that the Jewish psalms were illuminated by the light of Christ falling upon their pages. The liturgical year itself gave new meaning to the same psalm as it was selected on different occasions: for instance, the verse from Psalm 24 'Lift up your heads, O ye gates, and be ye lift up ye everlasting doors, for the King of Glory shall come in' takes on a new meaning according to whether it is sung at Christmas, to signify the entry of the Lord into the world, at Easter, to signify his descent into hell, or at Ascension, to acclaim his entry into the gates of heaven. The addition of other words could also interpret a psalm, the simplest being the conclusion of each psalm with the words: 'Glory be to Father, and to the Son, and to the Holy Spirit', directing the prayer of the psalm to the Trinity. Antiphons were used to bring out the Christogical meaning of each psalm in its context: that is, phrases were sung either before or during the chanting of the psalm, indicating its inner meaning. Psalter collects, prayers read at the conclusion of a psalm or group of psalms to direct prayer towards Christ, also interpreted the words of each psalm.

The monks at Jarrow used the psalter continually; Ceolfrith established there 'the same complete method of chanting and reading which was maintained in the older monastery',[14] and all the 22 foundation members were able to chant or read in church. There is little direct information about the Office in Anglo-Saxon monasteries. There are, however, certain influences that can be conjectured: the first is the Office as prescribed for other monastic houses, perhaps especially that outlined in the *Rule of St Benedict*. It is tempting to cut the Gordian knot and assume that Benedict Biscop and Ceolfrith used the complex arrangement of the psalms for the Office according to the *Rule of St Benedict*, but there is little evidence that it was any more than one rule among many which the abbots drew upon to organize life in their new monasteries. Moreover, the arrangement of psalmody in the *Rule of St Benedict* was specifically something left to the discretion of the abbot. Ceolfrith was well acquainted with Wilfrid's Ripon, where, according to Eddius Stephanus, Wilfrid had introduced the *Rule of St Benedict*, which included instructing the monks in how to 'make use of a double choir singing in harmony, with reciprocal responses and antiphons',[15] but he had begun his monastic experience in the Irish monastery of Gilling, and also knew the monastery of Botolph in Suffolk and another monastery in Kent, while Benedict Biscop knew the Offices at the monastery of Lérins, and at St Peter's Canterbury, as well as at the various monasteries and churches of Rome. Just how distinct the Offices in these places were from the Office in the *Rule of St Benedict* at that period is not clear, but it seems safe to assume that the whole psalter was recited each week, and that the major part of it was at the Office of Vigils during the night.

The church services at Wearmouth, whatever they had been like at the monastery's foundation, were further shaped by the second influence at Wearmouth-Jarrow, the customs of eighth-century Rome. In 679, Benedict Biscop and Ceolfrith had visited Rome together, and there Pope Agatho agreed to allow John, the precentor of St Peter's and abbot of the monastery of St Martin, to 'teach the monks of his monastery the mode of chanting throughout the year as it was practised at St Peter's in Rome'.[16] The cantors of the monastery therefore learned the distribution of the psalms, the order and manner of singing and reading aloud, the lessons, the texts of the antiphons and responses, and the cycle of feasts in use at St Peter's. They had not so much books as a performer, a teacher who passed on his understanding by singing not by writing. The basilica of St Peter was the focus of the devotion of pilgrims, and especially of the Anglo-Saxons, and the founders of Wearmouth-Jarrow could find no better model for their own devotions. St Peter's, with its clerical and monastic singers, had an Office established in the second half of the seventh century, and this was carried north by John. It was above all an audible Office, Scripture-based. This Roman tradition of chanting the psalms so that they could be heard and understood spread widely and later could be insisted upon as the true norm; at the Council of Clovesho, for instance, one chapter insisted that the psalter should not be sung 'to the tragic tone of the poets' but straightforwardly 'according to the Roman use', while another explained in detail the obligation upon monks and clergy to base their worship directly upon the psalter.[17]

There were also canticles, other sections of biblical material arranged for singing included in the Office. For instance it is clear that the Magnificat was sung at Vespers, since in a homily on the Virgin Mary Bede refers to it:

It has become an excellent and salutary custom in the church for every one to sing this hymn [the Magnificat] daily in the Office of evening prayer.[18]

Bede also commented on another canticle, an Old Testament text this time, the canticle of Habakkuk, which was used in the Office of Lauds as a psalm outside the psalter. Here also his interpretation of the words was predominantly Christological:

The canticle of Habakkuk, which you asked me to explain to you, dearly beloved sister in Christ, is chiefly a proclamation of the mysteries of the Lord's passion.[19]

How were these psalms and canticles sung? Presumably with the single voice of a trained cantor for the psalms, with the repetitive sentences of antiphons as a chorus, either at the beginning and end or repeated after each or several verses. Aethelwulf, describing the chanting a century later in a cell of the monastery of Lindisfarne, says of Sigwine the fifth abbot:

> When the reverend festivals of God's saints came round and when between two choirs in the church he [Sigwine] sang the verses of the psalms among the brothers, they rendered in song the sweet-sounding music of the flowing antiphon. And the lector, a man very learned in books, poured forth song to the general delight, singing in a clear voice. And when, as the day went on, they completed the singing of the mass, the brothers accompanied their spiritual father to the table with harmonious song. Moreover no man could describe fittingly how earnestly he desired to celebrate sacred solemnities with his monks at festivals, how the clergy rejoiced within their bounds, shaking the church they filled it with loud singing.[20]

Psalmody was not a new tradition in Bede's day in England; when Augustine came to Kent, he and his companions met in the church of St Martin to 'chant the psalms' first and then to 'pray, to say mass, to preach and to baptize'; Aidan and his companions 'occupied themselves either with reading the scriptures or learning the psalms'. It is no wonder that the Anglo-Saxons placed the psalms at the heart of their life in Christ.

The Anglo-Saxons knew the psalms and in their Christological aspect they formed the structure of their thought. The psalter was central for them because it spoke about Christ, both in church in the Offices and in solitary prayer alone. For them the knowledge of the psalter by heart was natural, one psalm being learned and repeated after another. Wilfrid had learned the whole psalter by heart at Lindisfarne, in the old version of Jerome; he was able to change the entire mental structure of his prayer when he was in Rome by learning by heart a second psalter, that of Jerome, *iuxta hebraicos*. It says much for his powerful intellect that he could do so. Bede also used the same two psalters, presumably both known by heart. As a child he was taught the Gallican psalter, that used in church, Jerome's first revision of the Latin psalter, and it was this that he quoted in his writings and also used in his *De Metris et Tropis*. On two occasions, however, he used Jerome's later version, made from the Hebrew, once for scholarly purposes and once for prayer. One manuscript of the psalter of unique importance was written during Bede's lifetime in his monastery at

Jarrow. This is the Codex Amiatinus, the oldest extant copy of Jerome's complete vulgate Bible, which has for its version of the psalms the third revision of Jerome, *iuxta hebraicos*. The three great pandects made at Jarrow under Ceolfrith may well have owed their text to Bede's scholarly eye; certainly his care for Jerome's text *iuxta hebraicos* was in line with the text of the psalter produced for that book. Two of the three books were placed in church for anyone to read at any time.[21]

Another aspect of the glory of worship was the presence in church of such magnificent books, whose illumination was as full of teaching as the words they surrounded. The Lindisfarne Gospels, for instance, epitomizes in itself the whole of Anglo-Saxon corporate prayer: the work of dedicated people supported by great generosity of wealth and goods as well as time, the intricate ornamentation of the pages of the Gospel showing at a glance the glory of God which was within its words. Augustine had brought with him such books as well as a cross and icons; it may be that the great Gospel book called 'St Augustine's' was brought by him or his immediate followers. The words mattered in two ways: partly because of what they had to say about the Gospel, but also because they were made and surrounded by beauty to indicate the reverence in which their content was held. The Anglo-Saxons found that the new world of books which the missionaries brought was another freedom, this time from limitations of time and space: by reading they expanded into the past, by writing into the future, outside their own limited area and in a new permanence. They used Latin, but soon created their own written language, and continued their love of poetry in this new vein. Bede tells the story of the cowherd of Whitby, Caedmon, who became the first poet in Old English whose works were written and have therefore survived. Caedmon sang about the content of Scripture, learned by heart and in English.[22] But the physical appearance of the books they themselves made emphasized in their services the beauty of holiness.

Corporate meeting places were not all indoors. There were also the stone high crosses where pilgrims could congregate and be taught by the intricate imagery of the carving before them, but the buildings were central. They were, as Gregory had said, for the people, and the people were bonded together by the celebration of the services of the Church there. The fact that they delighted to be there was made clear in the amount of land and goods given for the new buildings and the crowds who frequented them. Bede reflected a wider understanding than his own when he wrote that he found this corporate recitation of praise and prayers seven times a day not only a duty but a delight:

> When I was seven years old I was, by the care of my kinsmen, placed in the care of the reverend Abbot Benedict and then of Ceolfrith, to be educated. From then on, I spent all my life in this monastery, applying myself entirely to the study of the Scriptures, and amidst the observance of the rule and the daily task of singing in the church, it has always been my delight to learn or to teach or to write.[23]

Later Alcuin recorded a story that when Bede was asked why he was so diligent in attending Office in old age he said:

> I know that the angels visit the canonical hours in the congregation of the brethren. What if they do not find me among them? Will they not say, where is Bede? Why does he not come to the prescribed devotions of the brothers?[24]

This delight in worship extended beyond the glory of the places to the glory of sound. The Anglo-Saxons sang their prayers. Singing mattered; they were a singing people. James the deacon and John the archchanter taught the Roman ways of chanting:

> From this time also men began to learn throughout all the churches of the English the way of singing in church which they had hitherto known only in Kent. Excepting James ... the first singing master in the church of the Northumbrians was Aeddi surnamed Stephanus, who had been invited from Kent by the most reverend man Wilfrid, the first among the bishops of the English race who learnt to deliver the catholic way of living to the churches of the English.[25]

The offices remained in Latin, but they were of great value to those who could not read much Latin. For instance, the saintly King Oswald attended the longest of the Offices and found it a basis for private prayer:

> Very often he would continue in prayer from mattins until daybreak; and because of his frequent habit of prayer and thanksgiving, he was always accustomed, wherever he sat, to place his hands on his knees with the palms turned upwards.[26]

Bede provided an abbreviated psalter, with a verse from each psalm, which he recommended for secular devotion. The meaning of the Offices was rendered into and expanded in English for private meditation. There are prayers in English for the Office of Prime which show the Anglo-Saxons' inner understanding of the monastic Offices:

> In the first hour of the day, that is at the sun's rising, we should praise God and eagerly pray him that he, out of his tenderness of heart, illuminate our minds with the illumination of the true Sun, that is, that he by his grace so illumine our inward thoughts that the devil may not through harmful darkness lead us astray from the right path nor too much impede us with the snares of sin.[27]

What took place in these churches filled with so much devotion and love was the sanctification of time by the daily chanting of the psalms in the divine Office. But even more central was the celebration there of the eucharist. Bede was proud of the fact that he had been made deacon at an early age and then priest by Bishop John of Hexham, one of the saints of Northumbria, and with the care of his beloved abbot Coelfrith:

> At the age of nineteen, I was ordained deacon and at the age of thirty priest both times through the ministration of the reverend Bishop John on the direction of Abbot Ceolfrith.[28]

He expressed his reverence for the sacrament later when he wrote:

> Whenever we enter the church and draw near to the heavenly mysteries we ought to approach with all humility both because of the reverence due to the presence of the angels and because of the reverence due to the sacred oblation; for as the angels are said to have stood by the body of the Lord when it lay in the tomb, so we must believe that they are present at the celebration of the mystery of his sacred body at the time of its consecration.[29]

Such an approach shows that the celebration of the eucharist for the Anglo-Saxons was by no means a clerical formality. It was said of the hermit bishop Cuthbert that he was overwhelmed by it:

> Cuthbert was so full of penitence, so aflame with heavenly yearning, that when celebrating mass he could never finish the rite without shedding tears. But, as was indeed fitting,

while he celebrated the mysteries of the Lord's passion, he would himself imitate the rite he was celebrating, that is to say, he would sacrifice himself to God in contrition of heart. Moreover, he would urge the people who stood by to lift up their hearts and give thanks to our Lord God, himself lifting up the heart rather than the voice, sighing rather than singing.[30]

Here, the link between life and prayer, word and example, is again stressed.

It is not possible to say what texts were used in the sixth and seventh centuries in England for the celebration of the eucharist, but it is certain that whatever they used came in some form from Rome. Augustine and his companions, or the surviving British Church, used the basic eucharistic patterns known in Rome, and the Irish were equally eager to do the same and to keep up to date as far as possible with innovations there: in the *Life of St Bridgit*, written *c*.750, there is a story about this:

A holy man came to the house where Bridgit was praying and found her alone standing with her hands outstretched to heaven in prayer .. she said 'I heard masses in Rome at the tombs of Sts Peter and Paul and it is my earnest wish that the order of this mass and of the universal rule be brought to me'. Bridgit sent experts to Rome and from there they brought back masses . . . again after some time she said to the men, 'I discern that certain things have been changed in the mass in Rome since you returned from there. Go back again.'[31]

The old Gelasian Sacramentary of *c*.670 was perhaps nearest to the masses of Rome loved by Bridgit, Wilfrid and Benedict Biscop, with their sense of the unity of the whole Church in heaven and earth. And the use of this rite was allowed by Gregory the Great; he wrote to Augustine:

My brother, you know the customs of the Roman church in which, of course, you were brought up. But it is my wish that if you have found any customs in the Roman or Gaulish church or any other church which may be more pleasing to Almighty God, you should make a careful selection of them and assiduously teach the church of the English, which is still new in the faith, what you have been able to gather from other churches.[32]

Baptism, however, provided the Anglo-Saxons' first experience of corporate liturgy and this was from the first closely linked to the celebration of the feast of Easter:

> So Edwin with all the nobles of his race and a vast number of the common people, received the faith and regeneration by holy baptism in the eleventh year of his reign, that is in the year of Our Lord 627 and about 180 years after the coming of the English to Britain. He was baptised at York on Easter Day, 12th April, in the church of St Peter the Apostle, which he had hastily built of wood while he was a catechumen and under instruction before he received baptism.[33]

Baptism here was administered for the king in his newly constructed York Minster, but Paulinus also baptized in the river Glen near the royal palace at Yeavering:

> So great is said to have been the fervour of the Northumbrians and their longing for the washing of baptism ... that Paulinus spent thirty-six days there occupied in the task of instructing and baptising ... washed them in the waters of regeneration in the river Glen which was close at hand.[34]

As has been said, the date of Easter was of practical importance for the first Anglo-Saxon Christians, But more than that, the observance of Easter was to do with theology. Easter, the moment of attention to the passion and resurrection of Christ, was not just a feast on its own that could be celebrated at whim. On it hung the whole of the Christian year, with Lent beforehand, Pentecost afterwards and all the Sundays of the year linked into it. Nor was the date of the death and resurrection of Jesus arbitrary: it was a historical fact in time, and because of it all time was changed into a new configuration. Tradition had linked the date into the ebb and flow of the universe, of all creation, and with this deep sense of the centrality of Easter, it is no surprise to find that when Bede preached he explored the mystery of this feast with a personal intensity, bringing all his enormous learning and his skill as a preacher to bear on the expression of truths deeply felt and firmly held as the very source of life itself. Bede collected together fifty of his own homilies, and of these eighteen are connected with Easter. One is outstanding in its imagery and power, and was preached on the night of the Easter celebrations at Jarrow, between 703 when Bede was ordained priest and 735, the year of his death. It is possible that the monks of Wearmouth Jarrow had been taught the new Easter vigil ceremonies by John the archchanter who came there from Rome with the abbot Benedict Biscop in the year Bede entered the monastery. It may well be that he introduced there a form of the *Exultet* for Easter night; the main part of Bede's homily shows striking parallels with such a text. He took as a starting point Matthew 28.1–10, the visit of the women to the tomb, but the homily rises to eloquence not by expounding each part of that text in detail but by a paean of praise taking up the great images used for the understanding of the night's mysteries from the Old Testament, the Lamb and the night of the passover, both so familiar liturgically in the *Exultet* chant:

On this most holy night, dearest brothers, we have heard from the Gospel reading that our vigils are to be given over to the resurrection of our Lord and Saviour. It is right that out of our love for him we should celebrate this night with vigils and hymns, who out of love for us willed to spend it in the sleep of death and to be raised from death, as the Apostle says, 'he died for our sins and rose for our sanctification' (Rom 4.25; 1 Cor 15.3).

From the beginning of the creation of the world till now the course of time was so divided that day comes before night, as it was created in the beginning. On this night that order of time was altered by the mystery of the resurrection of the Lord. It was during the night that He rose from the dead and it was on the next day that He showed the effect of His resurrection to His disciples. As they wondered and rejoiced, He shared a meal with them, proving the truth of his power.

It was most fitting that night should be joined to the following day and the sequence of time so arranged that day would follow night. Once it was appropriate for night to follow day, for by sin mankind left the day of paradise for the night and suffering of this age. It is now appropriate that day should follow night, for us who through faith in the rising of Christ are led back from the night of sin and the shadow of death into the day of life which is Christ's gift.

So, my dearest brothers, since we know that this special night has been made into day by the grace of the Lord's resurrection, let us take the greatest care that no part of it become night within our hearts. Every part should be as light as day for us, especially now as we keep vigil with the devotion of worthy praise and are waiting with pure and sober conscience for the festival of the day of Easter when this vigil is ended . . .

The unspotted Lamb came and deigned to be slain for us, he gave his blood as the price of our salvation, and by undergoing death for a time he condemned the sovereignty of death forever.

The innocent Lamb was slain, but by a marvellous and longed-for display he effectively weakened the strength of the lion which had slain him, that had brought sin into the world.

It was the Lamb that restored us by his flesh and blood so that we would not perish, (that brought to naught) the lion that was roaring about us seeking whom he might devour.

It was the Lamb who placed the sign of his death on our foreheads in order to ward off the weapons of the death-bearing enemy and his minions by crushing the boldness of unclean spirits. He broke open the gates of hell and brought forth his chosen who were held there (although in a state of rest), and by his rising from the dead on this very night, he led them to the joys of heaven.

Let us therefore then, as is right, be mindful of our redemption and devote ourselves during this night to a worthy vigil to God, and pay attention to the prayers and holy readings that tell of the favours of grace bestowed upon us.

Let us celebrate the new people of spiritual adoption taken away from the domination of Egypt and given to the one true Lord at the font of regeneration.

Let us sacrifice to God anew as a way of advancing to salvation, the most holy body and blood of our Lamb, by which we have been redeemed from our sins.

And since we are made glad by this yearly solemnization of the mystery of our Lord's resurrection together with our own redemption, let us strive, dearly beloved, to take hold of these mysteries by the inner love of our hearts and always hold to them by living them out. Let us sometimes keep them, like clean animals chewing them over by murmuring them with our lips, sometimes by gathering them together in the inner chambers of our hearts. Above all let us take care so to live that we may deserve to behold with joy the outcome of our own resurrection also. . . .

He himself will lead us all into the dwelling place of heavenly peace which he promised to us of old where he lives and reigns with the Father in the unity of the Holy Spirit God throughout all ages.

Amen.[35]

Many phrases of this sermon call on the great images of the Old Testament, the lamb slain from the foundation of the world seen as the lamb sacrificed at the passover, becoming the central image for Christ in the liturgy of Easter night. Time was cancelled in this liturgical moment, when the English gathered in their churches. What was ordained within creation was now revealed as fulfilled in them; but it was never just a moment of vision — it was presented as liturgy meant to lead listeners into the holiness of life which issues from this moment of resurrection, indicating the path into glory opening at their feet each day thereafter.

The death and resurrection of Christ was central, then, to the corporate prayer of English Christians in the seventh century. On the edge of the Christian world, they went straight to the centre of the mystery of love, seeing through the pages of the 'holy white scriptures' the joy of a whole redeemed created order, drawn through man into the love, peace and unity of Christ. It was no use seeking another door, or delaying men by controversy about the way in. The stones of the archway should be firmly established and agreed upon so that they need no longer be regarded. Here was the secret door through which the soul could pass and go in and out and find pasture. This ability to walk with saints and angels in the light of Easter resurrection extended to the world of nature as well. Nature was on the whole menacing to pagans, but the Easter celebration was the centre of love and of delight in restored creation. It extended even to whales. When the romance of the *Voyage of St Brendan of the Isles*, the work of an expatriate Irish monk of the late ninth century, was composed, the monastic travellers westward always took a break from voyaging for the celebration of Easter. For the seven years of their journey, it was celebrated each year on the back of a whale. At first the whale, 'the greatest creature of the sea', was as unaware of his privilege as the monks, but when the monks lighted a fire on his back, the

46

whale swam away. Seven years later, however, he was more ready to co-operate:

> They found Jasconius in the usual place, climbed out onto his back and sang to the Lord the whole night and said their masses the next morning; after the last mass the whale swam away ... in a straight line toward the island of the bird and there they stayed until the octave of Pentecost.[36]

This picture of the celebration of the Easter liturgy on the back of a whale is more than a pretty conceit; it recalls the image of Jonah in the whale, used by the fathers as an image of Christ's descent into hell.

The importance of Easter for the English found a different and more tender outlet later in a tenth-century poem, *The Descent into Hell*, where the poet expressed exactly the sense of expectation, wonder and joy that our predecessors felt at the moment of Easter:

> For in the dawning there came a throng of angels; the
> rapture of those hosts surrounded the Saviour's tomb.
> The earthly vault was open; the Prince's corpse received
> the breath of life; the ground shook and hell's inhabitants
> rejoiced. The young man awoke dauntless from the earth;
> the mighty majesty arose victorious and wise.[37]

Notes

1 EHEP, Book 1, cap. xxvi, p. 77.

2 Ibid., Book 3, cap. lii, p. 221.

3 HA, cap. 5, p. 189.

4 Ibid., cap. 7, p. 191.

5 Dedication stone in the church of St Paul at Jarrow.

6 *Life of Ceofrith, Abbot of Wearmouth and Jarrow*, trans. D. S. Boutflower (London, 1912), cap. 14, p. 65.

7 Bede, *Commentary on Genesis*, 1, 12, 8–14.

8 Bede, *On the Temple*, trans. Sean Connolly (Liverpool, 1995), Book 1, cap. 1, p. 5.

9 Bede, *Commentary on Genesis*, III, ii, 631–46.

10 Bede, 'Homilies on the dedication of a church, in *Homilies on the*

Gospels, trans. L. Martin and D. Hurst (Kalamazoo, 1991), vol. 2, 24 and 25, pp. 255–71.

11   Ibid.

12   Ibid.

13   John Chrysostom, 'Panegyric on the Psalter' in *The Holy Psalter*, trans. L. Moore (Madras, 1966), p. xxv.

14   HA, cap. 16, p. 202.

15   *Life of Wilfrid*, cap. 14, p. 120.

16   EHEP, Book 4, cap. xviii, p. 389.

17   Canons of the Synod of Clovesho (747) in *Councils and Ecclesiastical Documents Relating to Great Britain and Ireland*, ed. A. W. Haddan and W. Stubbs (Oxford, 1871), vol. III, cap. 2, p. 366.

18   Bede, 'Homily in Advent', in *Homilies of Bede, op cit.*, vol. 1, Homily 4, p. 42.

19   Bede, *Commentary on the Canticle of Habakkuk*, CCSL 119B; cf. also trans. by Sean Connolly (Dublin, 1997).

20   Aethelwulf *De Abbatibus*, ed. A. Campbell, (Oxford, 1967), cap. 15, p. 40.

21   HA, cap. 15, p. 201; cf. *Life of Ceolfrith, op. cit.*, cap. 20, p. 69.

22   EHEP, Book 4, cap. xxiv, pp. 415–22.

23   Ibid., Book 5, cap. xxiv, p. 567.

24   Quoted by C. Plummer in *Bedae Historia Ecclesiastica Gentis Anglorum* (Oxford, 1896), vol. 1, p. xii.

25   EHEP, Book 4, cap. ii, p. 335.

26   Ibid., Book 3, cap. xii, p. 251.

27   'The Benedictine Office' in *Anglo-Saxon Poetry*, p. 539.

28   EHEP, Book 5, cap. xxiv, p. 567.

29   Bede, Homily 4, *Homilies of Bede, op. cit.*, vol. 2, p. 121.

30   VSC, cap. xvi, p. 65.

31   *Life of St Bridgit*, cap. 90, trans. Sean Connolly; quoted by Eamonn O'Carragain, *The City of Rome and the World of Bede* (Jarrow, 1994), pp. 1–2.

32   EHEP, Book 1, cap. xxvii, p. 83.

33   Ibid., Book 2, cap. xiv, p. 187.

34   Ibid., Book 2, cap. xiv, p. 189.

35 Bede, 'Sermon on the Easter Vigil', *Homilies of Bede, op. cit.*, vol. 2, 7, pp. 56–69.

36 'The voyage of St Brendan' in *The Age of Bede*, ed. D. H. Farmer (Harmondsworth, 1965), cap. 27, p. 244.

37 The descent into Hell in *Anglo-Saxon Poetry*, p. 392.

4

The companionship of heaven

'The heavenly host to be my guard'

The meetings in church of the community of Christians on earth were by no means the only way in which the Anglo-Saxons experienced their life in the body of Christ. From the first, Christianity was for them the opening of new and heavenly dimensions. When Paulinus finally obtained a hearing from the king's court after the time of his silent presence in Northumbria, praying with the Queen, it was this aspect of Christianity which most attracted the king's companions. King Edwin consulted his men about the idea of conversion and one of his thanes expressed his interest in Christianity by comparing the restricted view paganism had offered of this life with the new and liberating dimensions of the good news:

This is how the present life of man on earth, O king, appears to me in comparison with that time which is unknown to us. You are sitting feasting with your eaoldermen and thanes in winter time; the fire is burning on the hearth in the middle of the hall and all inside is warm, while outside the wintry storms of rain and snow are raging; and a sparrow flies swiftly through the hall. It enters in at one door and quickly flies out at the other. For the few moments it is inside, the storm and wintry tempest cannot touch it, but after the briefest moment of calm, it flits from your sight out of the wintry storm and into it again. So this life of man appears but for a moment; what follows or indeed what went before we know not at all.

50

*The bishops worship at
St Alban's tomb and pray for
his help against the Pelagians.
From the Book of St Albans.*

Sea creatures minister to St Cuthbert after a night praying in the sea.
From Bede's Life of St Cuthbert, University College MS165.

Guthlac attacked by demons.

Guthlac and St Bartholomew with demons.
Two roundels from Harley Roll no. Y6.

Cast of the Ruthwell Cross, Dumfriesshire, on display in Durham Cathedral.
A cast of the Bewcastle Cross, from Cumbria, is visible in the background.

If this new doctrine brings us more certain information, it seems right that we should accept it.[1]

This new dimension of heaven was thickly peopled already with saints: the calendar of the Church through the year commemorated the apostles and martyrs of the early Church, while in Britain they already had their own martyr, Alban, with his shrine as well as his feast day. The saints were around them and awaited them at death:

Christ is the morning star who when the night of this world is past will bring his saints to the promise of the light of life and everlasting day.[2]

The Anglo-Saxons learned to count death as a beginning for the Christian, not an end, and the work of God in them was seen as perfected in death. One of the attractions of Christianity for them was its perspective of a wider reality which lay around their lives. They were always conscious of being part of the Church of God, and aware of saints of the past linked with those of the present. The lives of saints, past and present, showed most of all to the new converts that life was open towards another dimension, that life on earth was the threshold of the kingdom of God:

All the rest and hope and joy of the elect is only in the future sabbath where those who in this life walk with the Lord humbly following his precepts, are taken up by Him into life of perpetual rest and do not again appear among mortals but live immortal with Him.[3]

We now sing the praises of his grace so that we may deserve to overcome and in the future never cease to sing them because we have overcome.[4]

The saints of the Bible were felt to be present in England and available for everyone at all times, since the English were a new people of God themselves. Especially they were aware of the presence of Mary the Mother of Jesus, the person who was closest to Christ. Pictures of Mary appeared in manuscripts and in carvings; the four main feasts of the Virgin, the annunciation, the nativity, the purification and the assumption were soon well established.[5] The basic prayer used in connection with Mary combined two lines from the Gospel of Luke, the greeting of the angel Gabriel, 'Hail Mary, full of grace the Lord is with you', with the greeting of Elizabeth, 'blessed art thou among women and blessed is the fruit of thy womb'. To this was later added a personal cry for help: 'pray for us'. But devotion, and indeed a sense of personal need for an intercessor and great protector, prompted elaboration of this basic theme. The *Book of Cerne* and the *Book of Nunnaminster* contain three early Latin prayers to Mary. Though they were English in composition, from the second half of the eighth century, they may reflect earlier material. The beginning of the most elaborate consists largely in an outpouring of praise which flows into a plea of eager and almost overwhelming trust:

> Holy, ever-virgin mother of God,
> happy, blessed, glorious and noble,
> untouched and pure,
> chaste and undefiled Mary,
> immaculate, chosen and beloved by God,
> Endowed with singular sanctity
> and worthy of all praise,
> the mediator for the whole world
> when faced with danger,
> hear, hear, hear us,
> Holy Mary, pray and intercede for us
> and do not scorn to help.
> For we trust and we know for certain
> that you can obtain everything that you wish
> from your son, our Lord Jesus Christ,
> the omnipotent God, king of all ages,
> who lives with the Father and the Holy Spirit
> without end. Amen.[6]

The second is much more elaborate, though with the same tone of personal love and dependence upon a loving patron in the midst of a world of terror:

> Holy Mary, glorious mother of God and ever-virgin,
> who deserved to give birth to salvation for the world,
> hear me and have mercy on me now and everywhere
> through the honour and glory of your most excellent
>   virginity.
> I pray to you humbly be my salvation and my helper
> before Almighty God and our Lord Jesus,
> that the kind shepherd and prince of peace himself
> may purify me from the stains of sins

and rescue me from the darkness of hell
and lead me into eternal life.
　　Through you, O most pure virgin Mary,
he came into this most impure world
and saved mankind with his blood
and rose from death and destroyed the locks of hell
and opened the doors of the heavenly kingdom,
may he in his mercy deign to save and cleanse and guard
　　me
and, after the end of this fading life,
may Jesus Christ our Lord
grant me some part of eternal happiness
in the fellowship of the saints.
To him be honour and glory
with the Father and the Holy Spirit
for ever and ever. Amen.[7]

In a later Anglo-Saxon poem the same love for and dependence upon Mary was expressed:

O splendour of the world,
the purest woman on earth of those that have ever been.
Lady of the heavenly host
and of the earthly orders
and of the dwellers in hell . . .
Now show towards us that grace
which the angel, God's messenger, brought to you.
Especially we citizens of earth pray for this:
that you will reveal to the folk that consolation,
your own Son.
Then we may all with one accord rejoice
when we gaze upon the Child at your breast.[8]

Mary, the angels and the apostles, especially St Peter, were seen as present helpers, but the prayers of the Anglo-Saxons also sought out more recent saints among the Anglo-Saxons themselves. There were soon those who were regarded as saints; their tombs were visited and their miracles announced. This sense of another dimension to life, proclaimed by preachers and witnessed to by neighbours and friends, is a fact of the utmost importance in understanding these new Christians and their way of living and thinking. The dimension of the early Church of the Mediterranean world was dear to them, and many went to Rome to be near the burial places of the apostles and martyrs, but the tradition of friendship with the saints was not entirely new nearer to home. There had already been Christian saints in Britain whose bodies were honoured before the Anglo-Saxon invaders arrived. There was, for instance, St Alban: they knew the story of the visit to Verulamium in the second half of the fifth century of Bishop Germanus of Auxerre. There a tribune and his wife brought their blind ten-year-old daughter to the bishop and asked him to pray for her healing:

> Germanus, full of the Holy Spirit, invoked the Trinity. Then he tore from his neck the little bag which hung down close to his side containing relics of the saints. Grasping it firmly he pressed it in the sight of all on the girl's eyelids; her eyes were immediately delivered from darkness and filled with the light of truth.

The story was told as an illustration of the illumination of the darkness of error, since the point of Germanus' visit was to clear up heresy, but it is also notable that this enlightenment was completed only with the physical touch of the relics of the saints. The idea of receiving bodily health by the touch of a saint was by no means new and it was to have a long history; here it was given new reality in Britain, and the power of Christ through the living saints was complemented by the power located in the relics of the dead. The content of the small bag of bones which Germanus carried was a personal possession, and was described as a link with the early Church existing in a physical, tangible form:

> Germanus had with him relics of all the apostles and martyrs, that is those who had known Christ in his earthly life and those who were closest to him by death like his.[9]

Furthermore, Germanus visited the tomb of the British martyr Alban, a layman who had hidden a Christian priest who was in danger of death and had helped him to escape his pursuers by taking his place and dying by the sword. The place of his burial had continued to be venerated. After praying, Germanus ordered the tomb to be opened so that he might place his precious gift in it:

> He thought it fitting that the limbs of the saints which had been gathered from near and far should find lodging in the same tomb seeing they had all entered heaven equal in

merits. When they were honourably bestowed and placed side by side, he collected a heap of soil from the place where the blood of the blessed martyr had been shed to take away with him.[10]

The Anglo-Saxons visited the tombs of dead saints, collected soil from them, and expected cures there; it was a personal and vivid experience of the surrounding life of heaven on earth. As Bede had explained, the world was in its sixth and last age, but alongside those living were the saints, also alive and awaiting the last day. It was to be expected that they would continue to care for those living and help them in life and in death.[11] Germanus was not the only missionary to bring relics to Britain from the Mediterranean world. When the English mission was under way and Augustine needed more helpers, Gregory the Great sent to him Mellitus, Justus, Paulinus, Rufinianus . . .

and he sent with them all such things as were generally necessary for the worship and ministry of the church . . . relics of the holy apostles and marytrs.[12]

Mellitus, Bishop of London, received further instructions from the Pope about these relics. In a letter with a message to Augustine, Gregory ordered the missionaries not to throw down the pagan holy sites, but only the idols in them:

Take holy water and sprinkle it in these shrines, build altars and place relics in them . . . on the day of the dedication festivals of the holy martyrs whose relics are deposited there, let them make themselves huts from the branches of the trees around the churches which have been converted into shrines and let them celebrate the solemnity with religious feasts.[13]

In the North, when the abbots Benedict Biscop and Ceolfrith visited Rome and Gaul, they returned with the spoils of great libraries, but also with relics of the saints of the early Church. In 674, for the foundation of his new monastery at Wearmouth, significantly dedicated to St Peter, Biscop brought

many sacred books and the holy relics of the blessed apostles and martyrs.[14]

From his fourth visit to Rome he brought back

an abundant supply of relics of the blessed apostles and
Christian martyrs which were to prove such a boon for many
churches in the land.[15]

The bones of the founders of the Church were to enrich the soil
of England with holiness; a gateway was there for men to go in
and out and find pasture.

The actual state of the physical remains of the new saints in
England were seen more specifically as a sign of the resurrection
and a pledge of the Kingdom. In the case of certain saints, their
flesh remained whole and incorrupt after death: Etheldreda, Cuthbert, Fursey, and the arm of St Oswald, for instance, were buried
but their flesh remained undecayed. It could be seen as a sign of
virginity of body during life following the example of Christ
himself, or, as a sign of the Kingdom of heaven made visible in
the flesh here and now.

Another side of this understanding of the burial of the saints is
the respect of the Anglo-Saxons for the bones of the 'new' saints
and the accounts of miracles at their tombs.The converts buried
their dead to await the resurrection rather than burning them, and
beside these bones the poor and sick were healed. The healing
power of prayer continued even more strongly in the place where
the earthly remains lay, already impregnated with the resurrection
life. The gate was not entirely closed when the saints had passed
through. Healing and blessing are bestowed, messages come back,
and saints come at death for each other. For instance, at death
the Abbess Torhtgyth of Ely said she saw and spoke with 'my
beloved mother Ethelburgh',[16] and Cedd was seen to come and
lead back to heaven his brother Chad at his death.[17] It was their
conviction that those who died were nearer to Christ and therefore more able to help others; the means were hidden and such
things were called miracles and signs.The great cloud of witnesses
was still close at hand and could be asked to intervene in earthly
affairs:

> Through the intercession of the saints who shine, not through
> their own power but from Him, Christ will be propitious to
> the faithful when they raise their minds to heavenly desires
> and recognise His glory in the words and deeds of those who
> have preceded them in the fight.[18]

Dead saints were powerful patrons, but there was also value in
the saints as example and encouragement:

Beseech the souls who have preceded you to heaven to aid you by their good example and by recalling to you the beginning, course and enduring of the road of virtue which they travelled.[19]

The point of accounts of posthumous miracles of the saints was to show that *in patria* they did not abandon those still *in via*. Those closer to Christ shared more in his power of love, not less, and miracles of love and grace and healing continued through death. This sense of the household of God on earth and in heaven was especially attractive to the Anglo-Saxons in their entry into this new religion; here their existing sense of the value of the kin-group was given a new and lasting dimension.

In accounts of saints' lives, the common opinion about events and people was constantly shot through with the inner meaning of Christian sanctity. It is very interesting that this allusive, sideways, oblique way of writing about people in fact brings them more vividly alive than any other way. The first-generation Christians in England, Hilda, Chad, Wilfrid, Aidan, Etheldreda and Cuthbert, were written about as saints, but this was not to make them seem formal bloodless characters; on the contrary, these *Lives* present pictures of them that print them on the mind's eye with vigour and vitality. Where Aethelfrith and Oswiu and even Raedwald, with all his buried treasures, could be forgotten, and belong essentially to the past world, the saints are not. Hagiography seen as poetry, as theology and even as art, retains its original purpose and fulfils it:

> Not everything has a name; some things lead us into a realm beyond words. Art thaws even the frozen, darkened soul, opening it to lofty spiritual experiences. Through art we are sometimes sent, indistinctly, briefly, revelations not to be achieved by rational thought.[20]

Perhaps it was not after all so strange that to see someone in their own chosen light, which was that of Christ, should make not for distance but for all the warmth and closeness of real holiness. The last point about the saints' lives is that they were never written nor intended for modern historians to take apart and utilize for their own ends; they were and are news from a far country and good news for those who listen 'in this vale of tears'.

For the Anglo-Saxons, heaven was no vague and distant future; it was an immediate and daily way of life, filled with friends. Each day could begin with a sense of the companionship of the saints and angels, as is seen in this prayer for morning:

> May we walk in prosperity this day of light:
> in the power of the most High God, greatest of gods,
> In a manner pleasing to Christ,
> in the light of the Holy Spirit,
> In the faith of the patriarchs,
> In the merits of the prophets,
> In the peace of the apostles,
> In the splendour of the saints . . .
> In abundance of peace,
> In praise of the Trinity,
> With our senses alert,
> With constant good works,
> With spiritual powers,
> With holy life,
> In these things is the journey of all labouring for Christ
> who leads his saints after death into eternal joy.
> That I may hear the voice of the angels,
> praising God and saying Holy, Holy, Holy.[21]

Notes

1 EHEP, Book 2, cap. xiii, pp. 183–5.

2 Bede, *Commentary on Revelation*, cap. 2, v. 28.

3 Bede, *Commentary on Genesis*, Book 2, p. 88.

4 Bede, *Commentary on Habakkuk*, p. 402.

5 Cf. Mary Clayton, *The Cult of the Virgin Mary in Anglo-Saxon England* (Cambridge, 1990), pp. 98–102; ch. 4, pp. 90–121 contains an excellent discussion of these Marian prayers and translations.

6 A. B. Kuypers (ed.), *The Prayerbook of Aedeluald the Bishop, commonly called Book of Cerne* (Cambridge, 1902) (hereafter called *The Book of Cerne*), no. 56, p. 154.

7 W. de G. Birch (ed.), *An Ancient Manuscript of the Eighth or Ninth Century Formerly Belonging to St Mary's Abbey or Nunnaminster, Winchester*, Hampshire Record Society (London and Winchester, 1889), no. 57, p. 114 (hereafter called *The Book of Nunnaminster*).

8 *Christ 1*, IV, *Anglo-Saxon Poetry*, p. 212.

9 EHEP, Book 1, cap. xviii, p. 68.

10 Ibid., pp. 59–61.

11 Cf. David Rollason, *Saints and Relics in Anglo-Saxon England* (Oxford, 1989).

12 EHEP, Book 1, cap. xxix, p. 105.

13 Ibid., Book 1, cap. xxx, p. 107.

14 HA, cap. 4, p. 188.

15 Ibid., cap. 6, p. 190.

16 EHEP, Book 4, cap. ix, p. 363.

17 EHEP, Book 4, cap. iii, p. 345.

18 Bede, *Commentary on Genesis*, Book 2, p. 135.

19 Bede, *Commentary on the Song of Songs*, Book 2, p. 215.

20 Alexander Solzhenitsyn, Nobel Prize Speech, 'On Literature', London, 1970.

21 *Book of Cerne*, no. 6, pp. 89–90.

5

Prayer alone

'Bright candles over the holy white scriptures'

Cuthbert joyfully entered into the remote solitudes which he had long desired, sought and prayed for.... There is an island called Farne in the middle of he sea ... it is shut in on the landward side by very deep water and facing on the other side, and on the seaward side by the boundless ocean ...[1]

There is in the midland district of Britain a most dismal fen of immense size which begins at the banks of the river Granta not far from the camp that is called Cambridge ... when Guthlac had heard about the wild places of this vast desert he made his way thither with divine assistance by the most direct route.[2]

Hermits existed in Anglo-Saxon England, as they did in the early church where the first Christian hermits gathered in Palestine and the deserts of Egypt.[3] The literature about the first hermits was well-known and influenced the lives of later solitaries, but it was not a straight path from Egypt in the fourth century to the English barbarians of the seventh. In between there were accounts of solitary life in Ireland, in Gaul, in Spain, in Italy, and hints of it in the earlier Roman British Christianity. Whatever the Anglo-Saxons and the Irish knew about the accounts of the Egyptian hermits, it is necessary also to remember that later accounts of the experience of solitude of, for instance, Benedict of Nursia, Martin of Tours and Columba of Iona may have been equally influential.

Two of the hermits of Anglo-Saxon England, Cuthbert of

Lindisfarne and Guthlac of Crowland, were the focus of especially good literary records, which provide the earliest sustained accounts of this way of life in England. There were other hermits, of course; there are glimpses in Bede's *Ecclesiastical History* of several either full-time or part-time hermits: Fursey, Aidan, Ultan, Chad, Herebert, Wihtberht, Fergild, Bartholomew. Some were Irishmen who lived as hermits in England, others were Englishmen who lived as hermits in Ireland; some withdrew into solitude for extended periods, others for life. But the most respected hermit among them was Cuthbert of Lindisfarne.

Cuthbert was born about 643, and grew up in Northumbria where Oswald was king and Aidan from Iona was preaching and teaching. He engaged in military service, perhaps against the pagan Penda of Mercia, but in the year in which Aidan died, he entered the monastery of Melrose as a novice. Some years later he accompanied the abbot Eata to Wilfrid's monastery of Ripon, but then went with Eata to Lindisfarne where Cuthbert became prior. In 676 Cuthbert retired to live as a hermit on Farne Island; nine years later, he was taken from his solitude and made bishop by Archbishop Theodore; two years later he resigned and returned to his island solitude where he died the following year, 687; he was still alive when Bede, his main biographer, went as a boy of seven to be a monk at Jarrow. Bede wrote about him in verse and in prose, and included a long account of him in his great historical work, the *Ecclesiastical History of the English People*. There was also an earlier account by an anonymous monk of Lindisfarne. The life of Cuthbert was translated into English and his story told in illuminations in manuscripts. After his death, his cult attracted a continuing and ever popular veneration (eventually centred at Durham). He remained the great saint of the north.

The other English hermit who attracted an extensive record was Guthlac of Crowland (673–714). Felix, a monk in East Anglia, wrote his life in prose, and the twelfth-century historian Ordericus Vitalis (1075–1142) included a masterly abbreviation of Felix's life, which he justly described as 'a lengthy book in somewhat obscure style', in his *Ecclesiastical History*. Guthlac was later the subject of poetry in two Anglo-Saxon poems, and like Cuthbert, his story was also later recorded in art, in roundels, which may have been sketches for a further record in glass. Born in 674 in the land of the Middle Angles, then under Aethelred, to a noble house, he occupied his youth in a martial career, leading his own band, fighting along the Welsh borders, with great enthusiasm and success; Felix says he was a kind of early Robin Hood, giving a third of the spoils he obtained back to those who had been robbed. At the age of 24, he began to consider death more seriously and this led him, overnight, to leave his followers and become a monk in the monastery of Repton. Some years later, he decided on a more solitary way of life and went to Crowland, where he lived until his death in 714.

A comment by Ordericus Vitalis at the beginning of his account of Guthlac links the Anglo-Saxon solitaries directly with the early traditions of monastic Egypt:

> I steadfastly believe that the holy deeds of the Angles and Saxons of England could be no less edifying to Northern Christians than the deeds of Greeks and Egyptians which devoted scholars have fully recorded in lengthy narratives that are freely studied and give much pleasure. Moreover I believe that little as these things are known among our own countrymen they must prove all the more pleasing and full of grace to men of ardent charity who lament their past sins from the bottom of their heart.[4]

What then were the 'holy deeds' of the English Cuthbert and Guthlac? They were Christian hermits just as the ascetics of early Egypt were hermits. What did the northern hermits have in common with those of Egypt?

A sense of the importance of the individual before God is the most obvious characteristic of solitary life, but it is based on an equally deep apprehension of the solid unity of all mankind. What happens to one happens to all, so that wherever there is that sense of reality which is repentance before God for one, the whole of humanity receives it. There was among the Anglo-Saxons a concentrated sense of the group: that is clear from their laws, their institutions, their art, their commerce. They lived by the kin-group, the unity of men with their lord, who was their chosen 'high king' and who served them in love and friendship. They found it possible to convert this into the Christian understanding of union between the Head and members in the body of Christ. Their sense of the group was strong; the value of each one before God needed more thought. The hermits took the value of the individual very much to heart and were themselves examples of it. They may have lived outside the normal course of Christian piety but the basis of prayer for them was liturgical and scriptural, as it was for everyone else. In the famous story of Cuthbert and the otters this is clearly illustrated. Going out at night to pray in the sea:

> There followed in his footsteps two little sea-animals, humbly prostrating themselves on the earth, and licking his feet they rolled upon them, wiping them with their skins and warming them with their breath.[5]

It sounds like an account of a walk on the beach at night, so often fruitful for the English — a man alone by the sea, singing to himself and taking a dip, with small furry animals rubbing round his ankles. How attractive; is this perhaps — and how consoling it would be — the spirituality of the Anglo-Saxon hermits? But this most private, intimate moment in the prayer of Cuthbert was not so superficial for either of his biographers when they placed over it the lens of the Scriptures. For the anonymous writer, Cuthbert was Daniel, thrown into danger of lust, as Daniel was thrown into the den of lions; and Cuthbert, like Daniel, was ministered to by the animals.[6] For the Fathers of the Church, Daniel was never just the eunuch of King Nebuchadnezzar; he was Christ, who 'thought it not robbery to be equal with God but emptied himself' (Phil 2) and came down, a new Daniel, into this animal den of the world. For Bede the emphasis was different though equally scriptural; he used the words of the Gospel spoken by Jesus to his disciples after the Transfiguration, 'Tell the vision to no man until the Son of Man be risen again from the dead' (Matt 17.9). In his commentary on the Transfiguration, Bede re-stated the patristic understanding of this moment of vision as the second epiphany of Christ, parallel to the Baptism of Christ in the Jordan, the two revelations of the Christ as the Son of God. The 'vision' seen on the shore of the North Sea centuries later was for Bede the same epiphany of God, by water and by light. It was a moment of such awe and terror that a secret observer, like the disciples, 'trembled in anguish all night long'. He had not been watching a man on a beach with his pets; he had seen the face of Christ in a man so transfigured in prayer that the right order of creation was in him restored. Cuthbert with the otters was an awesome sight: he was the New Adam, once more at peace with all creation, naming the animals who were once more in right relationshiop with man. Moreover, though his prayer was ascetic and solitary, it was made within a corporate setting: he came out to do it from of the abbey of Coldingham where liturgical prayer of Office and mass were continuously celebrated, and he returned to join in that prayer well before dawn.

The extremes of hermit life, particularly, have always attracted question. Those who refused all public duties, including preaching and teaching, who lived on the borders of society in extreme poverty, and who never washed, starved themselves, never held a conversation or opened a book from one year's end to another, provoked criticism at once, from politicians, from those concerned with good order in society, from monks who lived in communities and also from humanists. In the fourth century, Rutilius Namatianus wrote, when passing a place where a former young friend was living as a hermit:

> Driven by the furies, out from men and lands,
> a credulous exile skulking in the dark,
> Thinking, poor fool, that heaven feeds on filth.
> Himself to himself more harsh than the outraged gods.[7]

It was of course at times a perfectly valid criticism; the earliest reference to the ascetics in Roman law calls them 'anchorites', meaning those who did not fulfil their public duties; it required them to show that they were not simply drop-outs but engaged in serious spiritual work.

In the lives of Cuthbert and of Guthlac there is criticism, but not of this kind. There are many reasons for this. This way of life was new in Egypt and in direct conflict with a humanistic and cultivated society; in England they were a rough, tough lot who received hermit traditions along with everything else; it was all very odd to them, and this drawing to solitude no stranger than the rest. Moreover, three centuries of Christian thinking had justified the ascetic life to the educated and to the civic-minded, as the ideals of the desert were understood and popularized. The criticism made of Cuthbert and Guthlac continued a different theme found in the desert, that of jealousy and rivalry between the monks, practising a corporate way of life, and those leading a more extreme hermit life, which was felt as a rebuke and a challenge. This often came from those who disliked such austerity as making demands on themselves; such instances were also recorded in order to show the goodness of the hermits by contrast with their critics. The ways of monks in community and of hermits rarely went together smoothly; and in certain ways the hermit life was as alien to community life as it was to society at large. Cuthbert and Guthlac were not easy members of monastic communities. Guthlac at Repton after his conversion 'never again took any draught of intoxicating drink ... for this cause he was intensely hated by all the brethren who lived with him there'.[8] Cuthbert, transferred from Melrose to Lindisfarne in order to be Prior and reform the lives of the monks, not surprisingly did not find a universal welcome; 'for there were certain brethren who preferred to conform to their older usage rather than the monastic rule'.[9] In the desert the hermits hardly ever tried to live in monasteries; it was a totally different lifestyle; in England they were closer together in every way. But what differed most was the situation of love and service in a newly Christian country. Northumbria and East Anglia were recently converted; they were not the cultivated, long converted Roman colony of Egypt, where theology attained its highest point of sophistication in Alexandria. Such a society could afford to have desert fathers also. But in England there was no such living Christian tradition. The monks had also to be the educators, the teachers, the thinkers, the refiners of doctrine. They were consulted by kings as intimates: they were made bishops and were used to palaces. They were literate men, and the simplicities of the desert perforce took a new turn with their lives. It is remarkable that in spite of this many of them lived as solitaries and many more admired them for it as the heroes of the new people of God.

The overall tone of admiration for Cuthbert and Guthlac may also have been because the extremes of hermit life which aroused scorn among fourth-century observers most of all, were not practised in England. Neither Cuthbert nor Guthlac, for instance, imitated Symeon, who beginning at the age of eighteen stood on various pillars, of various increasing heights, for 47 years through 'snow, rain and burning sun', in the mountains behind Antioch, and died there in 459, or his disciple Daniel, who stood for years on a pillar outside Constantinople. When the young Daniel had been on his way to visit Symeon, he met a party of monks who said scornfully 'never has such a thing happened anywhere that a man should go up and live on a pillar'. Cuthbert might stand all night praying in the icy waters of the North Sea, but he came out again. The stylites did not; when Daniel froze one winter into a block of ice on his pillar the townsfolk did not take him down; they thawed him out where he was. The stylites are the extreme of solitude, literally suspended between heaven and earth, always awake and standing in prayer, and they have always caused especial amazement:

65

Why did Symeon sit like
that without a mantle
without a hat
in a holy rage
for the world to see?
it puzzles the sage
it puzzles me
It puzzled many a desert father
and I think it puzzled the good Lord rather.[10]

Such extremes were not found in the north: perhaps it was a matter of climate, or even good northern common sense.

They might not be stylites, but Cuthbert and Guthlac were uncompromising solitaries and their ascetic practices aroused wonder more often than criticism.To go all-out for something always stirs the imagination:

Now God be thanked who has matched us with this hour
and caught our youth and wakened us from sleeping,
with hands made pure, clear eyes and heightened power,
as swimmers into cleanness leaping.[11]

It can be love, war, sport, art, music, scholarship, but often it is the desire for God. There is this sense of freedom, of single-mindedness, of delight and desire in the early accounts of the desert fathers and also with the Anglo-Saxons. Antony, an eighteen-year-old farmer's son in Egypt, heard the Gospel read in church, telling him to go and sell all that he had; and he went and did it. The young Cuthbert, arriving at Melrose and handing his spear to a bystander to emphasize his change of life, was at the same moment; so was the young warrior Guthlac, when sleepless with anguish over tales of the deaths of kings and the fleeting nature of riches he lay awake until

the winged birds chirped their morning song . . . he rose and bade his companions choose another leader for he declared that he had devoted himself to the service of God.[12]

Like those of the monks of Egypt, the lives of Cuthbert and Guthlac aroused wonder but they also provoked curiosity and a kind of religious greed to profit by them. Visitors came to them as holy men for advice and most of all to ask for their intercession. This had also been the case in Egypt: the writer of *The History of the Monks of Egypt* was full of the greatest praise for the worldwide results of their prayers:

> It is clear to all that dwell there that through them the world is kept in being and that through them too human life is preserved and honoured by God.[13]

Because of this confidence in their friendship with God, Cuthbert and Guthlac were frequently consulted by visitors, often by kings and queens, and even more often asked for their prayers. To preserve the essence of solitude while keeping charity with individual visitors was hard enough. What was even more difficult was the fact that the Church as an institution also admired the hermits and regarded this way of life jealously and tried its best to use the hermits; they wanted to ordain them as priests and bishops, to use their reputation in defence of orthodoxy, to draw their lifestyle into a place where they would give edification to many, even though in the process they might destroy them. The danger for the hermits from the institutional Church was that it was trying to take them away from solitude and tame them with both education and ordination. Cuthbert received education at Melrose and to his great sorrow later became a bishop and left his solitude for a time; at his election 'he could by no means be dragged from his place ... until at last they drew him shedding many tears from his sweet retirement'.[14]

The way of life of Guthlac and of Cuthbert, as distinct from the opinions of others about them, had much in common with that of earlier hermits. For instance, they expressed content with and indeed love for their way of life. It was, after all, a way of life voluntarily chosen, not imposed. This was no romantic love of nature but a delight in discovering the place where they ought to be, as a Shaker song puts it:

> When you find yourself in the place just right
> You'll be in the heaven of love and delight.

It is easy to see that something all hermits had in common was a delight and happiness and longing for what they were meant to be doing. When Antony reached the inner mountain, the utter solitude, he was 'as if stirred by God [and] fell in love with the place ... looking on it as his own home, from that point forward he stayed in that place.[15] The hermit Paul, when he discovered in the desert an abandoned mint, mysterious, eerie, strangely beautiful in the moonlight, intensely remote, settled there for 113 years and called it 'this beloved habitation'.[16] Guthlac on Crowland 'loved the remoteness of the spot seeing that God had given it to him and vowed with righteous purpose to spend all the days of his life there',[17] and Cuthbert 'joyfully entered into the remote solitudes which he had long desired sought and prayed for'.[18] A poet-hermit summed up this delight:

Alone in my little hut without a human being in my company, dear has been the pilgrimage before going to meet death . . . My creator to visit me, my Lord, my King, my spirit to seek him in the eternal kingdom where he is.[19]

Secondly, though accounts of hermits, including Cuthbert and Guthlac, contain descriptions of dreams and visions, they are mainly about inner temptation, not revelations of glory or wisdom. It was a plain, practical life. And the hermits when glimpsed are plain unaffected men, with a humour and discreetness that is as attractive as it is traditional. When Antony met the old hermit Paul in the desert, Paul made a joke before letting him enter his cell, and there was no record of great flights of spiritual exchange in their talk. Antony later summed it up by saying 'I have seen Paul in paradise'. Cuthbert prayed secretly in the sea at night and rebuked the monk who wanted to see wonders and followed to spy on him, enjoining total silence about what he had seen. Guthlac in the fens underplayed any prophetic gifts others discerned in him, giving accounts only of temptation in prayer.

The hermit life might be embraced with love but it was no walk through a nature reserve or stay at a holiday camp.The hermit had deliberately chosen to live at the limits of existence, a human person containing both heaven and earth, with the angels and with the beasts, a mediator of all creation. It was not an easy position but one of constant conflict within the self. Cuthbert, questioned about his last silent days on Farne, said only 'My adversaries have never persecuted me so frequently during all the time I have been living on the island as during the past five days'.[20] Elsewhere he said about his temptations by the demons:

How many times have they cast me down headlong from this high rock, how many times have they hurled stones at me as if to kill me. But though they sought to frighten me away by one phantasmal temptation or another, and attempted to drive me from this place of combat, nevertheless they were unable in any way to mar my body by injury or my mind by fear.[21]

The temptations of Guthlac were described in terms similar to those of Antony the Great:

> He suddenly saw the whole tiny cell filled with horrible troops of foul spirits ... ferocious in appearance, terrible in shape, with great heads, long necks, thin faces, yellow complexions, filthy beards, shaggy ears ... when dawn was at hand and the sun drove the shades of night from the sky, the same athlete of Christ having won the victory over his enemies, stood giving thanks to Christ.[22]

Cuthbert's temptations were described in biblical terms, those of Guthlac in more lurid images, but under the drama of both lay a more common human experience: 'he began to despair so utterly that he thought he had undertaken an infinite and unsupportable labour'.[23] This sense of total despair, at one's inability to love or be loved, is a basic human experience which most of all linked the hermits to their compatriots:

> the pain in which I am drowning is no doubt the same river of pain which is closing over millions of other men at this moment. So what? You're alone, completely alone, that's the only sure thing.[24]

The hermits chose to endure this awareness of emptiness within and to discover, if not its resolution, at least that it is not the 'only sure thing'. The endurance of solitude by the hermit issued not in despair but in a genuine if discreet love of others: they discovered that, in fact, relationship with all creation is possible when the central relationship with Christ is established. Bede wrote of Cuthbert:

> yes, and the very sea itself, as well as the air and fire as we have shown, did honour to the venerable man ... for if a man faithfully and wholeheartedly serves the Maker of all created things, it is no wonder that all creation ministers to his commands and wishes.[25]

Felix had similar comments to make about Guthlac:

> The excellence of his charity abounded to all creatures so that even the birds of the untamed wilderness and the wandering fishes of the muddy marshes would come flying or

69

swimming to his call as if to a shepherd and they were even accustomed to take from his hands such food as the nature of each demanded ... for if a man faithfully and wholeheartedly serves the Maker of all created things, it is no wonder that all creation ministers to his commands and wishes.[26]

The hermit became the new Adam through whom the world was restored. Antony visiting Paul had met centaurs and fauns asking for prayer and baptism; lions came running from the wilderness to bury Paul in the sand at his death. Antony and Paul were both fed by bread dropped by a raven. Cuthbert had his otters and his ravens, while the life of Guthlac is full of the song of birds. At the other end of the scale, moreover, Guthlac had St Bartholomew as a close and personal friend. Angels flashed in and out of the air, surrounding the hermits with so great a company. The angels, the demons and the saints surrounded them while the birds, fish, animals, all were once again renamed by the new Adam and human relationship was restored in the light of love.

The hermits of Egypt and of England had, of course, the traditional pre-Christian ascetic practices of silence, solitude, poverty, prayer, work, fasting and vigil in common. They followed the traditional ways of life of those who are both celibate and chaste, explorers of inner space, both male and female, alone and completed by God along the patterns of the Gospel. What amazed their biographers was what they did not have, but what motivated them was the drawing of this love and the voice of this calling. On the other side of silence and non-speech they were hearing words so dear, a music so clear that they had no inclination to listen to chatter; eating the bare minimum of food, they had no room for more because they fed on the bread of heaven, a food so sweet they had no hunger for earthly bread; they walked away from companionship because they had another with them who was more dear. Guthlac expressed this by saying that every morning and evening God sent an angel to talk with him. Cuthbert might arrange a Christmas dinner for his visitors, but he himself preferred to be alone with God for the feast. The food of the Christian hermit, whether in Egypt or England, was the presence of Christ encountered through the Scriptures: they knew the psalter and a great deal of the rest of the Bible by heart, and this was their source of life. Cuthbert said that his memory served him instead of books, while Guthlac diligently learned the Scriptures before going into solitude:

I wish, O Son of the Living God, ancient and Eternal King,
for a secret hut in the wilderness that it may be my dwelling..

A beautiful wood close by around it on every side, for the
nurture of many voiced birds, to shelter and hide in it . . .

Then, bright candles over the holy white scriptures.[27]

What was different most of all from Egypt was the circumstances in which this was lived out. In England, the sea became
the desert since their physical situation was on an island. Whereas
in the sandy desert of Egypt Antony loved the place because
'below the hill there was water perfectly clear, sweet and very
cold and beyond there were plains and a few untended date
palms',[28] Guthlac and Cuthbert had no need to find more water.
Guthlac, reaching the island in the middle of a marsh, lived in an
old barrow with a hut on top of it. Cuthbert likewise found
solitude in an island in the midst of the sea, where he built a two-
roomed hut of stones and wood roofed with timber and straw. An
island like Britain is not the same as a desert; there the sea
becomes the desert:

Delightful I think it to be in the bosom of an isle on the peak
of a rock, that I might often see there the calm of the sea.

. . . That I might see its heavy waves over the glittering
ocean as they chant a melody to their Father on their eternal
course.[29]

Finally, in the accounts of the death of the hermits, all the
sources agree. After all, how else does one talk about resurrection
except in the images of the New Testament, a body risen, a garden
of flowers, of sweet scents, of white garments, of angels and of
light? In each case there is silence about the actual moments of
death, but for all of them there are the images of resurrection and
heavenly life breaking through. Perhaps the one thing that is
distinctive in the English hermits is the idea that the flesh of the
hermit will not decay but immediately present the appearance of
heavenly life. After the death of Cuthbert:

On opening the sepulchre, they found the body intact and
whole as if it were still alive.[30]

When they opened Guthlac's tomb, 'They found his body whole
as if it were still alive'.[31]

The incorrupt bodies of English saints were seen, as has been
said, as a sign of the immediate nature of the resurrection of the

body. And it is this life-giving presence of Christ which is central to these stories of hermits.

It is not the lion which makes the martyr or the desert or sea that makes the hermit, and it was not their external austerities that endeared hermits to the English. It was the fact of lives lived out sincerely according to the principles which all had received. Whether it was in a general way or a particular way, the hermits based their lives on biblical sources. They were motivated by the sense of another country that is in the heart of everyman: it was not the only nor yet the most usual way of living towards God, but it was one way in which to do it, when touched by the single desire for God alone. At the same time as Cuthbert and Guthlac were living and Bede and Felix were writing, the tall sculptured stone crosses were being made, the most famous of which are those at Bewcastle and Ruthwell. At Ruthwell, the image of the meeting of the hermits Paul and Antony is among the carvings; they are breaking between them the bread of heaven, as they are on at least ten of the later Irish high crosses. They suggest that the hermit life was seen as integral to Christianity in the British Isles, and also that the basic image on which such lives were built was that of the Cross. Paul and Antony, Cuthbert and Guthlac were not the only kind of Christians, but they were seen in Anglo-Saxon England as the heroes:

> many conditions of men there are thoughout the world beneath the heavens which belong in the number of the saints and accordingly we may duly serve in any of them ... some dwell in desolate places and of their own volition seek out and settle homes in shadowy retreats; they await the heavenly abode ... these are the tried warriors who serve a king who never withholds the reward from those who persist in loving him.[32]

Notes

1   *Two Lives of St Cuthbert*, ed. and trans. B. Colgrave (Cambridge, 1940) (Bede's *Life of St Cuthbert*, hereafter referred to as VC), cap. xvi, p. 215.

2   Felix, *Life of St Guthlac*, ed. and trans. B. Colgrave (Cambridge, 1956) (hereafter referred to as *Guthlac*), cap. xxiv, p. 67.

3 Cf. *Sayings of the Desert Fathers*, trans. Benedicta Ward (Oxford/ Kalamazoo, 1973).

4 Ordericus Vitalis, *Ecclesiastical History*, ed. and trans. M. Chibnall (Oxford, 1969), vol. 2, p. 325.

5 VC, cap. x, p. 189.

6 'Anonymous life of St Cuthbert' in *Two Lives of St Cuthbert*, cap. iv, p. 83.

7 Rutilius Namatianus, *De Reditu Suo*, ed. P. J. Vessereau (Paris, 1933), trans. Helen Waddell, *The Desert Fathers* (London, 1936), p. 12.

8 *Guthlac*, cap. xx, p. 84.

9 VC, cap xvi, p. 211.

10 Phyllis McGinley, 'Simon Stylites' in *Times Three* (New York, 1975), p. 47.

11 Rupert Brooke, 'Peace' in *Collected Poems of Rupert Brooke* (London, 1924), p. 5.

12 *Guthlac*, cap. xix, p. 93.

13 *Lives of the Desert Fathers*, Benedicta Ward and Norman Russell (Oxford/Kalamazoo: 1981), p. 50.

14 VC, cap. xxiv, p. 239.

15 Athanasius, *Life of St Antony*, trans. R. T. Meyer (London, 1950), p. 68.

16 Jerome, *Life of St Paul the Hermit*, trans. H. Waddell, *The Desert Fathers*, pp. 41–53.

17 *Guthlac*, cap. xxv, p. 89.

18 VC, cap. xvii, p. 215.

19 'The hermit', poem 224 in *A Celtic Miscellany*, trans. K. H. Jackson (Harmondsworth, 1951), p. 281.

20 VC, cap. xxxvii, p. 277.

21 VC, cap. xxii, p. 229.

22 *Guthlac*, cap. xxxi, pp. 101–7.

23 Ibid., cap. xxix, p. 97.

24 Jean Anouilh, *Eurydice* (Paris, 1947), translated by the author.

25 VC, cap, xxi, p. 225.

26 *Guthlac*, cap. xxxviii, p. 121.

27 'The Wish of Manchan of Liath', poem 223 in *A Celtic Miscellany*, p. 280.

28 *Life of St Antony*, caps 49, 50, p. 62.

29 'St Columba's island hermitage', poem 222 in *A Celtic Miscellany*, *op. cit.*, pp. 279–80.

30 VC, cap. xxii, p. 292.

31 *Guthlac*, cap. li, p. 161.

32 *Guthlac A* in *Anglo-Saxon Poetry*, p. 251.

6

Anglo-Saxon prayers

'Christ within me'

The prayer offered and shared by the Anglo-Saxons in church with the saints and the prayer in solitude of the hermits were essential parts of the spirituality of Anglo-Saxon England. But what can be known about the prayers of Anglo-Saxon men and women when they were neither in church nor in a hermitage? There are some texts of prayers from this early period both in Latin and in Anglo-Saxon, and there are descriptions that indicate how people prayed, though it is never at any time a simple matter to know just what converse a person has with God. There were two texts which formed the basis of their private prayers, first, the psalms; and secondly the Our Father.

The psalms for the Anglo-Saxons were not just formal and corporate prayers; they provided Christ-centred texts which could be the basis of the content of their own devotion. The psalms would be known by heart from constant hearing in church, so becoming a physical part of each person, as an almost unconscious layer of prayer. The use of the psalms in the liturgy shaped the minds of the Anglo-Saxons throughout their lives more consistently than any other text. Personal meditation on the psalms is part of the long tradition of compunction: *compunctio cordis*, the interior aspect of prayer, that bright sorrow without which Christianity is merely a religion and a rite.

In the monasteries of Anglo-Saxon England, as among the first Christians, the psalter was used in a special way as the basis of prayer. The psalter was learnt by ear by men for the most part unable to read and without books; it was learnt by heart and therefore the obvious way to remember it was by one psalm after another. And because the monks were not only praying when they met in church, but following a life of prayer, the interiorization of the psalms was as natural as breathing, especially in the monasteries which were the centres of Christianity throughout the island.

Early theologians had commented on the meaning of the psalms for Christians, notably Jerome, Augustine and Cassiodorus.These were known at least to some of the Anglo-Saxons but it was not the grammatical exegesis of Jerome, the doctrinal interpretations of Augustine or Cassiodorus or any combination of both that was basic to the Anglo-Saxons' love of the psalms. It was very often not the literal, grammatical meaning nor the Christological doctrinal meaning only of a verse that they drew out, but its precise application to their own lives. The whole Bible was for them by one author, God, and the psalms were relayed by one author, David, but they were not an end in themselves; through them, God spoke to Christians now, the living word of God, clarifying the present and illuminating the one praying.

This style of prayer was basic to their love of the psalms. It was often in the crucial moments of death that the familiar words recurred as prayer in individuals. Many men have died with the psalms as the basis of their prayer: Augustine, for instance, in the fourth century, had the seven Penitential Psalms always before him at death and Teresa of Avila in the sixteenth century repeated over and over again the verse from Psalm 51, 'a broken and a contrite heart, O God, thou wilt not despise'. The basic reason for the fact that the psalms strengthen dying men is surely that the evangelists offered the highest possible instance of their use, when Christ on the Cross used the words of Psalm 22, 'My God, my God, why hast thou forsaken me' and, for his last and ultimate prayer, Psalm 30, 'Father, into thy hands I commend my spirit' (Luke 23.46). There were many instances of this final moment illuminated by the psalms among the Anglo-Saxons.Three examples must suffice.

At the end of the life of Cuthbert of Lindisfarne, the monk Herefrith found the hermit-bishop alone and in great mental as well as physical pain:

> I went in about the ninth hour and found Cuthbert lying in a corner of his oratory opposite the altar; so I sat down by him.

He did not say much because the weight of his affliction had
lessened his power of speech.... He passed a quiet day in
expectation of his future bliss until the evening; and he also
continued quietly in prayer through a night of watching. But
when the usual time arrived for night prayer, he received
from me the sacraments of salvation and strengthened himself
for his death, which he knew had now come, by the communion of the Lord's body and blood. Raising his eyes to heaven
and stretching out his hands aloft, he sent forth his spirit in
the very act of praising God, to the joys of the kingdom of
heaven.[1]

On the mainland in the abbey of Lindisfarne the brothers
waited to see the beacon blaze on the island to tell them that
Cuthbert had died. And when it happened they were chanting
Psalm 59, 'O God thou hast cast us out and scattered us abroad',
as part of the ordinary course of the psalms at the Night Office.
They saw in it a personal significance. For Cassiodorus, this psalm
was a description of how God had shattered the pride of those
bound in sins and would recall them into a strong city which was
Christ. For Augustine, the casting out and scattering abroad could
apply to any temporal suffering endured for Christ, but was
especially appropriate to that of the martyrs. The psalm was used
liturgically, since it formed a natural part of the sequence of
psalms chanted one after the other at vigils for that night. But in
the dark days that followed at Lindisfarne, what was worth
recording in detail was how the context of contemporary events
was lit up by its phrases, illuminating daily experience in Northumbria in their own time. After Cuthbert's death, there was
trouble at Lindisfarne, such trouble that it could be expressed
only by those words of despair, 'O God, thou hast cast us out and
scattered us abroad'. It is not clear why there was such a falling
apart, but it seems that many monks left Lindisfarne; some of
them left in distress. It also seems that with the appointment of
Eadberht as bishop a measure of stability returned. 'Turn us
again', they seemed to have been crying after the death of
Cuthbert, and that restoration happened. The psalm was given an
immediate application to human events, beyond its grammatical
and Christological meaning. There is a sense of wonder in the
account of this psalm, that it should have so exactly expressed
events and emotions.

Another death also was accompanied by a psalm which was

seen as significant, that of the founder and abbot of Wearmouth-Jarrow, Benedict Biscop. First, there was a moment of touching personal love between two abbots when they were fatally ill and unable to say the psalms in choir; the brothers formed two small choirs and sang the usual psalms antiphonally at their bedsides until towards the end a moment of friendship united them:

> Both Benedict and Sigfrid were worn out with their protracted illness; they knew they were near to death and would never be fit to rule the monastery again. Their weakness gave scope for the strength of Christ to be perfected in them, but physically they were so weak that one day, when they both wished to see each other and talk before they died, Sigfrid had to be carried on a stretcher to the room where Benedict lay on his pallet. Their attendants set them side by side with their heads resting on the same pillow, a sight to move you to tears. Though their faces were close together they had not enough strength to turn to kiss each other and had even in this to be helped by the brothers . . .[2]

Four months later, Benedict Biscop was at the point of death:

> the brethren gathered in church awake during the dark night praying and singing psalms, relieving the sorrow they felt at their father's passing by constant praise of God.

Again, when he actually died their internalization of the psalter found significance in the psalm they were singing at that moment. This was Psalm 82, of which the second verse was 'For lo, thine enemies make a murmuring and they that hate thee have lift up their head'. Jerome had interpreted this psalm as about either the Church and heretics or the Israelites and their enemies, both literal and spiritual; Cassiodorus gave it a doctrinal meaning about Christ and the soul; for Augustine, it was a psalm concerning the Church and the world, or Christ and evil. But for the monks of Jarrow its meaning was deeply personal when related to the death of their abbot. Aware of previous interpretations of the psalm they were yet alert to see a vigorous and lively meaning here in relation to present events; their devotion was not antiquarian, nor limited by previous commentary, but made them ready to pray the texts through present life and experience in the light of Christ. Their familiarity with this kind of interpretation shed a discreet light upon the death of Benedict Biscop; it was a prayer for deliverance in extreme danger at death. The cell of the abbot, who was dying after great suffering, did not contain a peaceful scene such as the death of Caedmon, Drythelm, Boisil, or Bede himself; for this much-travelled, energetic and able ex-thane death was a bitter agony of soul as well as body. And Benedict Biscop was no less a saint for that prolonged anguish, terror and indignity which all men fear most in dying.

When Bede himself was dying, his former pupil Cuthbert, later Abbot of Jarrow, wrote to Cuthwine, another Saxon monk:

> Daily he gave us lessons who were his pupils and spent the rest of his day in chanting the psalter as best he could. . . . When he woke up he would at once take up again the familiar melodies of scripture.[3]

The theme of Bede's death was not prophecy of disaster or lament for sin; well aware of the terrors of death, he still sang psalms of thanksgiving, and, just as when he was a boy at Jarrow in the beginning with Ceolfrith, so at the end the antiphons were on his lips along with the psalms: 'He used to sing the antiphons for his own comfort and ours.' When he reached the point of death, he chanted the familar conclusion of every psalm by which each was always given a Christian and Trinitarian meaning:

> and so upon the floor of his cell, singing 'Glory be to the Father and to the Son and to the Holy Spirit' and the rest, he breathed his last.

To use the words of the psalms to articulate present terror and grief, as well as joy and wonder, was for the Anglo-Saxons to discover through the psalms hope beyond hope. As a cry of protest against the inhumanity of man the words of the psalms were always especially appropriate. Whether the horror was personal or cosmic, whether it was Christ on the Cross, genocide among nations, exile from a monastic home, the loss of someone held dear, or the personal anguish of dying, the words of the psalms expressed that for which they had no words and at the same time linked them into the life of redeeming love: 'Out of the deep have I called unto thee, O Lord, Lord, hear my voice', 'I am so fast in prison that I cannot get out', 'O deliver me from them that persecute me for they are too strong for me', 'my God, my God, why hast thou forsaken me?', could all become the words of immediate and heartfelt prayer.

The man who was most enthusiastically vocal in his praise of the psalter as a book for prayer was also an Englishman, also from the north; this was Alcuin (735–804), a pupil of the school of Egbert at York. Alcuin recommended the psalter earnestly as the basis of intimate prayer, carrying its use into another mode of self-awareness:

> If any oppressive sorrow has come upon you, either by an injury brought on by others, or by a besetting fault, or by an overwhelming domestic loss, if you grieve for any reason at all, do not murmur against one another or place the blame on God, but rather pray with psalms to the Lord lest the sadness of the world which is death swallow you up; drive the destructive sickness of grief from your heart by the frequent sweetness of the psalms.[4]

There was in Alcuin a more interior interest in the person praying and his needs, and not only expressions of fear but also of love and praise. The words of the psalms were to him the perfect expression of human praise, wonder, love and delight as well as sorrow, repentance and at times revolt and protest, though with a strong sense also of the external form of the psalms:

> In the psalms if you look carefully you will find an intimacy of prayer such as you could never discover by yourself. In the psalms you will find an intimate confession of your sins, and a perfect supplication for divine mercy. In the psalms you will find an intimate thanksgiving for all that befalls you. In the psalms you confess your weakness and misery and thereby call down God's mercy upon you. You will find every virtue in the psalms if you are worthy of God's mercy in deigning to reveal to you their secrets.

The psalms were not a limitation but a freedom; they were a preparation for receiving the word of God in ways beyond human emotions and needs:

> When the voice of psalmody acts through the intention of the heart, then a way to the heart is prepared for Almighty God, so that He may fill the innermost mind with the mysteries of prophecy or with the grace of compunction, as it is written, 'Whoso offers me praise, he honoureth me; and I will show him the way of salvation of God'. So in the sacrifice of divine praise we are shown the way to Jesus, because when through the psalms the heart is filled with compunction, a way is made by which we come to Jesus. Certainly it is appropriate that

when all things are recollected in the mind it cleanses itself and breathes praise of God in the spirit, so that the heavens may be revealed to it.

The psalter was for Alcuin also a summary of the revelation and prophecy contained in the rest of Scripture; it was the whole Bible compressed into one text, a pantechnicon for the Christian for the whole journey of life:

> In the psalter to the end of your life you have material for reading, scrutinizing and teaching; in it you find the prophets, the evangelists, the apostles and all the divine books spiritually and intellectually treated and described and the first and second coming of the Lord in prophecy. You will find both the incarnation and the passion, resurrection and ascension of the Lord and all the power of the divine words in the psalms if you peruse them with the intent of the mind and you will come by the grace of God to the marrow of intellectual understanding.

Outside as well as inside the monasteries such use was made of the psalter. Bede had made a selection of single verses from each psalm which he formed into an abbreviated psalter, which could easily be known by heart by anyone.[5] This way of using extracts from the psalms for the basis of compunction in prayer had a central place in the articulation of devotion in England, from the seventh century to the eleventh, when a new age found another channel for that same compunction of heart in lengthy meditations which provided other words for the same emotion of prayer. This personal and interior prayer was a strong current flowing in a great tradition: when in the eleventh century another man renowned for piety, Anselm, Archbishop of Canterbury, was asked to provide such 'flowers from the psalms' for a great and devout lady, he sent her something more. What caught and held the interest of the eleventh century was not selection from the psalms, but his own majestic prayers and meditations which gave a new form to the prayer of compunction and tears.[6]

With the psalter in their memories as the content of living prayer, the Anglo-Saxons also had a framework for prayer and this was provided by the Our Father. In his letter to Egbert of York at the end of his life, Bede recommended changes and improvements in the Christian life of his contemporaries, and among his motivations was a concern that the Our Father and the

Creed should be known by heart by all Christians in English, thus providing the basic framework of both belief and prayer. As a biblical scholar, he knew the textual problems presented by the two versions of the Our Father provided in the Vulgate Gospels of Matthew and Luke, and in his commentary on the *Gospel of Luke* he presented a scholarly commentary on the Lord's Prayer, dealing with its form rather than its content. About 70 per cent of Bede's writings were commentaries on the Bible, which he intended for the use of the clergy who had to teach and preach, and had no access to books. Bede himself had a library unparalleled in the north of Europe and he used it diligently in order to convey what was of value in the Christian tradition of biblical commentary to others for their use, so it is not surprising that when he commented on the Lord's Prayer he made use of Augustine's earlier comments in his *Enchiridion ad Laurentium*. In his preface to his commentary on Luke he wrote to Bishop Acca:

> Having collected from everywhere the works of the Fathers who are as it were the most skilful craftsmen in so great a task, I have tried to consult diligently what blessed Ambrose, what Augustine, what Gregory, the apostle of our race, and the most watchful in accordance with his name, what Jerome, translator of sacred history, and what the rest of the fathers thought and said about the words of blessed Luke.[7]

In his commentary on the Lord's Prayer in Luke, after he had commented on the story of Mary and Martha at Bethany, symbolizing the active and contemplative ways of prayer, Bede continued:

> After the account of the two sisters, who signify the two ways of life in the church, it is not without meaning that it is said that the Lord himself prayed and taught his disciples to pray, because the prayer which he taught both contained in itself the sacrament of life and we men cannot obtain the perfection of our lives except by prayers; and also because repeatedly Luke described the Saviour as praying, which prayer he carried out not for his own sake but for ours; he suggests that that which he had asked was granted when having finished his prayer when his disciples asked him to teach them how they ought to pray. And he said to them: when you pray, say 'Our Father, which art in heaven, hallowed be thy name, thy

kingdom come, thy will be done, on earth as it is in heaven; give us this day our daily bread; and forgive us our trespasses as we forgive those who trespass against us and lead us not into temptation but deliver us from evil'.

In the Gospel according to Matthew the Lord's Prayer seems to contain seven petitions, three of which ask for eternal things, the remaining four for things temporal, though the last four are necessary antecedents to the attainment of the eternal goods. For when we say 'Hallowed be thy name, thy kingdom come, thy will be done on earth as it is in heaven' which some understand not unfairly as in body as well as in spirit, we ask for things which are to be enjoyed for ever; they are indeed begun in this world and grow in us as we go forward, but we hope to possess them wholly in another life forever.

But when we say, 'Give us this day our daily bread, forgive us our debts as we forgive our debtors, lead us not into temptation but deliver us from evil' who does not see that these things belong to the needs of this present life? In that eternal life for which we hope in future, the hallowing of God's name, and his kingdom, and the doing of his will in our spirit and our body will be perfected and endure forever. But our daily bread is so called because here there is always need for as much nourishment as both flesh and spirit demand, whether bread is understood spiritually or carnally or in both senses.

It is here too that we need the forgiveness for which we ask, since it is here that we commit all sins. It is here that there are the temptations that allure or drive us to sin. In short, the evils from which we want to be delivered are here, but in the next world there will be none of them.

But the evangelist Luke in his version of the Lord's Prayer includes not seven but five petitions. Not of course that there is any discrepancy but that Luke briefly shows the way in which the seven petitions of Matthew are to be understood. For though the name of God is to be hallowed in spirit, God's kingdom will come with the resurrection of the body. So Luke omits the third petition altogether to show that it is a sort of repetition of the first two. He then adds three others, one for daily bread, another for pardon of sins, a third for deliverance from temptation. That which Matthew puts as the last petition 'but deliver us from evil' Luke has omitted to show us that it is included in the previous petition about temptation. Indeed Matthew himself says 'but deliver' not 'and deliver' as if to show that the petitions are virtually one, not do this, but this. So that everyman may understand that he is delivered from evil by the fact of not being led into temptation.[8]

Bede's interest in the Lord's Prayer was not only that of a scholar but that of a monk. At Jarrow he was accustomed to the daily public recitation of the Lord's Prayer in Latin as part of the Office, as a section on the *Rule of St Benedict* suggests was common monastic practice:

> Certainly the celebration of lauds and vespers must never pass by without the superior reciting the entire Lord's prayer at the end for all to hear, because thorns of contention are likely to spring up. Thus warned by the pledge they make to one another in the very words of this prayer 'forgive us as we forgive' they may cleanse themselves from this kind of vice. At other celebrations only the final part of the Lord's prayer is said aloud that all may reply 'But deliver us from evil'.[9]

In his homilies and certain other writings he gave more devotional and interior comments on the Lord's Prayer, which were continued fifty years later by Alcuin, who became the central figure in the Carolingian renaissance at the court of Charlemagne. Like Bede, in his comments clause by clause he was concerned with content and meaning for the praying heart. His commentary is part of his work on the liturgical prayer of the Church, while Bede's comments are embedded in biblical exposition and homily: together the comments of these two Anglo-Saxons show their interior understanding of the Lord's Prayer in particular and also reflect that of their contemporaries, inside and outside the monasteries.

Our Father

And here the priest joins his hands and says 'Let us pray' and the church prays with the priest not in voice but in heart. In silence the heart cries to God in the ears of God. 'Our Father': the only begotten Son has made us sons of God by the font of new birth and the spirit of adoption ... so when He says 'when you pray, say Our Father' we are acting out of obedience not out of boldness. The sons must imitate their good father as Isaac imitated Abraham and Jacob Isaac as he said, 'Be ye holy because I the Lord your God am holy' (1 Peter 1.16).

Who art in heaven

The name of God is holy so why do we say hallowed be thy name? When we are born again by water and the spirit at baptism we are made holy in the name of God almighty when the priest says, I baptise you in the name of the Father and of the Son and of the Holy Ghost. So we pray that the holiness that was created in us then at baptism by the invocation of God may fill us for ever so that we may not corrupt it but just as we were once made holy so we may remain so for all eternity.

OR: that we may understand how holy Thy Name is, that is it is holy in all things and when we remember such holiness we should be afraid to sin.

OR: if anyone is a good Christian, he does good work ... so that the name of Christ is hallowed in his servants; so we pray that the name of God may be made holy by being praised and glorified in all our works. For whatever we do that is good is for his praise but whatever we do that is bad brings scorn upon him.

Thy Kingdom come

It also sometimes happens that we seek things entirely related to salvation with our eager petitions and devoted actions and yet we do not immediately obtain what we ask. The result of our petitions is postponed to some future time as when we daily ask the Father on bended knees saying 'Thy Kingdom Come' and nevertheless we are not going to receive the kingdom as soon as our prayer is finished but at the proper time.

What is the kingdom of God? Eternal blessedness as it is said, 'Come, ye blessed of my father' (Matt 25.34).

OR: the almighty God reigns in his chosen ones by faith, hope and love and all good works. The devil reigns in us by greed, drunkenness, hatred and all evils; so we pray that it may be the Lord who reigns in us by righteousness and not the devil by sin.

Thy Will be done:

We are admonished to include this even in the Lord's prayer, 'Thy will be done'; namely not our own. For if we remember as well that saying of the Apostle 'We do not know what to pray for as we ought' (Rom 8.26), we understand that sometimes we beg for things opposed to our salvation and are very appropriately denied these things which we ask for earnestly by him who desires what is useful for us more truly than we do. That is, in the angels who never sinned who do your will and their service is always acceptable to you; so let your good will be done on earth so that your servants may be pleasing to you.

By heaven we understand the Lord Jesus Christ, by earth, the church. We know that as a man is to a woman, so is heaven to earth. From heaven the church receives all its fruitfulness, 'every good and perfect gift cometh from above' (James 1.17). Just as your will is done in heaven which is Christ so may it be done in the church which is his body.

OR: as it is done in the heaven of just men, so may it be done also in the earth of sinners by their repentance.

OR: as in our souls so also in our bodies. As angels live in heaven, so live men on earth who rejoice in the praises of God, in the pure heart of psalmody. No mortal man can fully declare the virtue of the psalms. In them are the confession of sins, the tears of the penitent, sorrow of heart. Here is foretold all the dispensations of our redemption, the wondrous delights of heaven's mirth. Here shall you find the Incarnation, Resurrection, and Ascension of the Word of God.

Give us this day our daily bread

By breaking the bread which he gave to his disciples the Lord designates the opening of the secret meanings by which the world was to be nourished unto perpetual salvation. The bread of life to the perception of whose inner meanings we cannot ourselves penetrate, should be laid bare to us by him.

The untaught sought the food of the word of God by which they could be refreshed unto the virtue of good actions and lacking teachers found no-one to open to them the secrets of the scriptures and instruct them in the way of truth.

We must not fear that if we seek the gift of love from the Lord with deep devotion and say from the depth of our hearts 'Give us today our daily bread' he will let our hearts be narrowed into the rigidity of hatred. [Samuel after anointing Saul] 'Then thou shalt go forward from thence and thou

shalt come to the plain of Tabor and there shall meet thee
three men going up to God at Bethel, one carrying three
kids, another carrying three loaves of bread and another
carrying a bottle of wine; and they will salute thee and give
thee two loaves of bread which thou shalt receive at their
hands.'

The disciples received bread from the hands of the Lord
when he opened their understanding that they might understand the Scriptures.... We are being nourished on food
roasted on the gridiron when we understand literally, openly
and without any covering the things that have been said or
done to protect the health of the soul; upon food cooked in a
frying pan when by frequently turning over the superficial
meaning and looking at it afresh we comprehend what there
is in it that corresponds allegorically with the mysteries of
Christ, what with the condition of the catholic church, and
what with setting right the ways of individuals; and afterwards
we search in the oven for the bread of the Word when by
exertion of mind we lay hold of the mystical things in the
Scriptures, that is, upon matters hidden above which as yet
we cannot see but which we hope we will see hereafter.

Give us this day our daily bread: bread means all that is
necessary for us in food, drink, clothing, to be given us today
in this temporal life.

OR: by daily bread we can understand the body and blood of
Christ of which he said 'Unless you eat of this bread' (John
6.54). Let us pray that in receiving his body and his blood
that by that which we see with our eyes we may receive that
which we do not see, that is, Almighty God, 'whoso eateth
my flesh and drinketh my blood remains in me and I in him'.
Where it says 'daily' we cannot refer to the reception of
communion since there are those think they cannot receive it
daily because of sin, while others do this remembering that
the Lord said to Zacchaeus 'Today I must stay in your house'
and he received him joyfully' (Luke 19.5). Those who feel
they cannot do this may say with the centurion 'Lord I
am not worthy to receive you under my roof' (Matt 8.5); I
will come another day.' But Augustine says of this kind of
humility, 'Brothers, I am pleased with your humility in fearing
to receive the body and blood of the Lord, but it would be
better if you were to receive it as cleansing for your sins and
as repentance.'

OR: by bread we also understand the word of God speaking in the law, the prophets, the psalms and the Gospels. In the time of our mortal life, refresh us with the teaching of the holy Scripture so that as our body is refreshed by earthly food, so this spiritual food may refresh our souls to love and knowledge of you.

Forgive us our trespasses as we forgive those who trespass against us

The person who has been cleansed in the baptismal font and has received pardon for all his sins has no need to be cleansed again, moreover he cannot be cleansed again in the same way. He finds it necessary only to have the daily defilements of his worldly life wiped away by the daily forgiveness of his Redeemer. His whole body together with its actions is clean with the exception only of those things which cling to the mind because of the necessity of temporal cares. For the cleansing of such daily pollution we say daily in prayer 'forgive us our trespasses as we forgive those who trespass against us'.

He who taught us to pray about our offences and sins promised that his fatherly mercy and pardon would follow.... In this life he forgives the elect their daily and individual sins without which we cannot live in this life. The blood of Jesus his son cleanses us from all sins. For the sacrament of the Lord's passion has equally freed us from all sin in baptism and the grace of our redeemer forgives whatever we have committed through daily frailty after baptism particularly when in the midst of the works of light which we do with humility we daily confess our errors to him when we receive the sacrament of his blood when after forgiving those who trespass against us we entreat that our trespasses be forgiven us, when mindful of his passion we may gladly bear all adversities.

Those who are about to say to Him in prayer 'and forgive us our trespasses as we forgive those who trespass against us' have fulfilled the commandment in which he says 'when you pray, grant pardon if you have anything against anyone'. Charity covers a multitude of sins especially insofar as someone says truthfully to God 'forgive us our trespasses as we forgive those who trespass against us'. And indeed all good works which we profess wipe away and cover the faults we commit but this is said particularly about the charity by which we give to our neigbours those things which were given to us, because it is most righteous in the sight of God that it be measured out to us according to the measure of devotion which we have ourselves measured. We are debtors to God in two ways, either by doing what he has forbidden or by not doing what he has commanded. Do we love God and our neighbour as he commanded? we are debtors, sinners. Do we honour our parents? we are debtors and sinners. Do not kill, do not commit adultery, do not swear, do not give false witness, we are daily offending against what he had commanded and so we are his debtors. If we would be forgiven by the Lord we must forgive our brother from the heart; or else we are doubly disobedient both by our own sins and by not loving our neighbour as we are commanded in not forgiving him.

And do not lead us into temptation
There is one kind of temptation which is a testing, as God tempted Abraham to prove his faith; there is another temptation which is of the devil, for 'God tempts no one' (James 1.13). We pray not to be led into the evil of temptation beyond what our frailty is able to bear. God is said to lead us into temptation when he does not free us from temptation.

But deliver us from evil
that is, from the devil and the pains of hell and all adversity in this world.

Amen
to signify and confirm this prayer.[10]

By such comments on the inner life through the structure of the Lord's Prayer, the spirituality of Anglo-Saxon Christians was formed, as priests and teachers absorbed these views and communicated them. Bede in particular was concerned that this treasury of prayed theology should be available to form the basis of prayer for the whole people of God, not just those scholars and monks who knew Latin, and he wrote about this at the end of his life to Bishop Egbert of York, an old friend and colleague:

In preaching to the people, this message more than any other should be proclaimed; that the catholic faith, as contained in the Apostles' Creed and the Lord's Prayer which the reading of the Gospel teaches us, should be deeply memorized by all who are under your rule. All who have learnt the Latin tongue by constant reading have quite certainly learnt these texts as well, but as for the unlearned, that is those who know their own language only, make these learn the texts in their own language and sing them accurately. This should be done not only by the laity still settled in secular life but also by clerks and monks who are not expert in the Latin language. For thus it will come about that the whole congregation of believers learns how to be full of faith and how it must protect and arm itself against the attacks of unclean spirits by firm belief; thus it comes about that the whole chorus of those who are praying to God learns what should be specially sought from God's mercy. That is why I have frequently offered translations of both the Creed and the Lord's prayer into English to many unlearned priests.... Moreover the custom of repeated prayer and genuflections has taught us to sing the Lord's prayer more often.[11]

Bede's translations of these texts do not survive, but there is a later Anglo-Saxon translation and expansion of the Lord's Prayer:

Pater Noster qui es in caelis
Father of mankind, I pray for your solace, holy Lord, you who are in the heavens.

Sanctificetur nomen tuum
May this your name be hallowed now, fast fixed in our intellects, redeeming Christ, fast established in our bosoms.

Adveniat regnum tuum
May your kingdom come to us mortals, Wielder of mighty powers, righteous Judge, and may your sublime faith remain in our hearts for the span of our lives.

Fiat voluntas tua sicut in caelo et in terra
And may your will be fulfilled among us in the habitation of the kingdom of earth as clear as it is in the glory of heaven, pleasingly beautified forever in eternity.

Panem nostrum cotidianum da nobis hodie
Give us now today, Lord of men, High King of the heavens, our bread, which you sent into the world as salvation to the souls of mankind: that is the pure Christ, the Lord God.

Et dimitte nobis debita nostra
Forgive us, Guardian of men, our guilts and sins, and pardon our crimes, the body's wounds, and our wicked deeds, although we often offend against you, the almighty God, in your mercies.

Sicut et nos dimittimus debitoribus nostris
Just as we pardon on earth their crimes those who often do wrong against us, and do not think to accuse them of their evil deeds, in order to merit eternal life.

Et ne nos inducas in temptationem
Do not lead us to punishment, into the grief of affliction, nor to the testing, redeeming Christ, lest we, devoid of grace, become out of enmity estranged from all your mercies.

Sed libera nos a malo
And also free us now from the evil of every fiend; we in our hearts shall zealously speak thanks and glory, prince of the angels, true Lord of victories, because you by your mighty powers mercifully freed us from the bondage of hell-torments.

Amen.
So let it be.[12]

Prayer for the Anglo-Saxons was therefore linked with the Scriptures, especially, but not exclusively, with the psalms and the Our Father. But prayer could rise up spontaneously from other parts of the Scriptures. During his commentaries, Bede's consideration of the text often formed itself into his personal prayer:

Almighty God, have mercy upon your suppliant for I am not as so many of your servants are, sublime through contempt of the world, glorious in the merits of their righteousness, angelic with the adornment of their chastity, nor am I even such as those who after public crimes by doing penance have become devoted to you. Indeed if by the aid of your grace I have done anything that is good, I do not know from what motive I have done it, nor with what severity it will be judged by You.

O Almighty God, open wide my heart and teach it by the grace of your Holy Spirit to ask for what is pleasing to you. Direct my thoughts and sense so to think and to act that by a worthy manner of life I may deserve to attain the eternal joys of the heavenly kingdom. Direct my actions according to your commands so that, ever striving to keep them in my life, I may receive for my deeds the eternal reward.

Would, Lord Jesus, that also in our times you would bestow such grace upon your faithful that they would do without not only the seeking of carnal pleasures but even sometimes the daily reception of food through eagerness to learn from their teachers.

I thank you O Jesu, for making blessed in heaven those who die in you on earth and how much more those who lay down their blessed lives in and for your faith.

Glory always to God and the Lord our Saviour both now and for ever and when amidst the pressures of adversity we still live in the body and are struggling apart from him, and particularly then, when the long desired of all nations shall come and deign to enlighten us by the vision of his presence. Meanwhile, we deserve to sigh for him and earnestly sing, because one day in your sight is better than a thousand elsewhere.

And now that at length so great and hazardous a labour has been complete I beg and pray that if anyone shall think this little work of mine worth reading or copying out, they will also remember to commend to the Lord the author of the work for I have not laboured for myself alone but also for them. May I in return be rewarded by the vows and prayers of those who have benefited by my toil and may they by their good offices cause me to gain the right to and fruition of the tree of life, the odour and good report of which I have in some measure communicated to them.

And thou great Father of light, from whom cometh every good and perfect gift, who hast given to me, the humblest of thy servants, the desire and means to see the wondrous things of thy law, and the grace worthily to bring forth out of the treasure of the prophetic volumes things new and old for the use of my fellow-servants: remember me, O my God, for good.

At the end of his *Ecclesiastical History* he wrote:

I pray you good Jesus, as you have graciously granted me sweet draughts of the Word which tells of you, so you will of your goodness grant that I may come at length to you the fount of all goodness and stand before your face forever.[13]

Similarly, a prayer was included by Eddius Stephanus in his *Life of St Wilfrid*:

O Christ, eternal Light, never deserting those who acknowledge you, whom we believe to be the true light which 'lightens every man that comes into the world', who in the beginning marked with fiery glory the hour of your future servant's birth, when he came out of his mother's womb; now as he prayed in the darkness of his prison cell you sent an angel to visit him and bring him to light just as when your apostle Peter was imprisoned in chains by wicked Herod. To You be glory and thanksgiving. Amen.[14]

The Old English poem *Christ 1* is a meditation in Anglo-Saxon on the antiphons used during Advent for the Magnificat and shows how deeply the Anglo-Saxons absorbed the new Christian Latin texts from the liturgy and expanded them to express their own culture and belief:

O Dayspring Refulgence of eternal light and sun of righteousness, come and illumine those who dwell in darkess and the shadow of death.

O Dayspring, brightest of angels sent to men upon middle earth and the sun's righteous radiance, of a brilliance exceeding the stars, you by your own self continually illumine every hour.

O Emmanuel, our King and Lawgiver, Hope of the nations and their saviour, come and save us Lord our God.

Come now, high King of heaven, in your own person, bring salvation, life, to us weary thralls in torment, overcome by weeping, by salt bitter tears. The cure for our excessive hardships belongs wholly to you alone. Seek out us melancholy captives here and when you return hence do not leave behind you a multitude so great, but in kingly manner show mercy upon us, Saviour Christ, Prince of heaven, and do not let accursed devils have dominion over us. Impart to us the everlasting joy of your glory so that those may worship you, glorious King of the heavenly hosts, whom once you fashioned with your hands. In the heights you will for ever remain with the Ruler and Father.[15]

Notes

1 VC, cap. xxxix.

2 HA, cap. xiii, p. 198.

3 *Letter of Cuthbert on the Death of Bede*, EHEP, p. 581.

4 Alcuin, *De Psalmorum Usu Liber*, preface: PL 101, col. 465.

5 Benedicta Ward, *Bede and the Psalter* (Jarrow, 1992).

6 *Prayers and Meditations of Anselm of Canterbury with the Proslogion*, trans. with introduction Benedicta Ward (Harmondsworth, 1970), pp. 26–82.

7 Bede, 'Letter to Acca', Preface to *Commentary on Luke*, p. 5.

8 Bede, *Commentary on Luke*, p. 227.

9 *Rule of St Benedict*, cap. 13.

10 Our Father: combined comments from Bede and Alcuin from various parts of their works.

11 Bede, 'Letter to Egbert' in EHEP, ed. J. McClure and R. Collins, p. 346.

12 *Anglo-Saxon Poetry*, p. 534.

13 Bede, EHEP, Book V, cap. xxiv, p. 571. The other quotations are taken from several of Bede's commentaries on the Bible.

14 Eddius Stephanus, *Life of Wilfrid*, in *The Age of Bede*, cap. 36, p. 144.

15 *Christ 1*, in *Anglo-Saxon Poetry*, pp. 208–9.

7

Prayer and the Cross

'Christ was on the Cross'

We and our fathers have now lived in this fair land for nearly three hundred and fifty years and never before has such an atrocity been seen in Britain as we have now suffered at the hands of a pagan people.... The church of St Cuthbert is spattered with the blood of the priests of God, stripped of all its furnishings, exposed to the plundering of pagans, a place more sacred than any in Britain.... A terrifying judgement has begun at the house of God where rest some of the brightest lights of all Britain.[1]

This was how Alcuin, the leading scholar of the court of Charlemagne and pupil of Egbert of York who had been the friend and disciple of Bede, wrote on hearing of the sack of Lindisfarne by the Danes in June 793. Bede had died in 735, and nearly fifty years later his monastery as well as the monastery of St Cuthbert had been plundered by the Danes and its monks scattered: the *Anglo-Saxon Chronicle* says, 'Northumbria was miserably ravaged by the heathen, and Ecgfrith's monastery of Jarrow was looted'.[2] Disaster: how did the twofold love of God that the Anglo-Saxons experienced with such eagerness and vigour, whether as a nation or as individuals, survive total and agonizing destruction? Did it make any difference to the sucessors of the first converts that they were in a situation of war rather than peace, death rather than life, limitation rather than freedom? What was the meaning in their lives then of the cross which Augustine had held before them, gleaming in silver, as a sign of victory? It is here that the real seriousness of the Christian life was made plain. The testing of pain has always been central to the experience of Christ. In his last illness Bede's companions said that he ' was 'filled with joy and gave God thanks that he had been found worthy to suffer this illness'.[3] This apprehension of the Cross as the central point of union with Christ and therefore not something to be avoided or confused with any kind of comfortableness was brought out starkly in a radio programme when an interviewer asked Lord Hailsham if, when he lost his wife by a tragically early death, he found consolation in his strong religious belief; he replied 'None whatsoever; the cross was applied without palliative.' That is exactly what the first missionaries hoped would be the Anglo-Saxon Christian stance: the Cross was not something that made them feel better, nicer, more comfortable, more victorious, more reconciled to tragedy, better able to cope with life and death; it was rather the centre of the fire in which they were to be changed. How far they had understood this was a question that was asked many times. The recommendation of Gregory the Great that externals could be kept if transfigured by inner holiness was too often reversed into the more comfortable ways of keeping charms and magic, where the external objects were held to have power; power at first to be exercised by the controlling person, but soon dominating and restricting life into a narrow selfishness. With this in mind, I would like to look finally at two situations in England in which 'the cross was applied without palliative'. This understanding of disaster as victory and not defeat seemed so vital to two Englishmen that both attributed the decline of Christianity and the desolation of their country to a failure to grasp that very point. I would like to discuss the comments of both these men, Bede and Alfred the Great, and also to investigate why it was that both turned for a remedy to the teaching of Gregory the Great. I have deliberately chosen Alfred the Great, a king and a married man, along with a simple monk who never held any position of power, to underline the fact that the way of the Cross is common to all and not for any special group.

In the last years of Bede's life he became deeply concerned about the state of contemporary English Christians and made this the subject of earnest discussion with his former pupil Egbert, then Archbishop of York, whom he visited in 733. The next year, too ill to travel again, Bede instead wrote to Egbert, warning him about the dangers surrounding him and suggesting remedies. He was not concerned about any open return to paganism, but he wrote most sternly about the dangers of a half-baked Christianity, of simply adding on Christian externals to an already comfortable life. There were three sides to this. The poor were neglected, the clergy were both greedy and irresponsible, and the freedom to establish monastic centres was being flagrantly misused as an excuse for wide-scale tax-evasion:

> Many villages and hamlets of our people are situated in inaccessible mountains and dense woodlands where there is never seen for many years at a time a bishop to offer any service or bestow any grace, though not one among them however is spared from rendering his dues to the bishop. . . . Certain bishops serve Christ in such a fashion that they have with them no men of learning or good life but rather those who are given over to laughter, jests, tales, feasting and drunkenness. . . . Those who are totally ignorant of monastic life have received under their control so many places in the name of monasteries that there is a complete dearth of places where the sons of nobles and veterans can receive an estate . . . those in such monasteries freely devote themselves to lust and fill those places with all kinds of crimes.

In fact, he concludes, there are those who claim the name of Christian but without the Cross:

> There are those who who are known to go through the wide gate that leads to destruction and the broad way through their whole lifetime and trouble not to withstand or resist for the sake of heavenly reward their desires of body or mind in the smallest matters.[4]

Bede had not been unaware of such matters earlier; when he wrote the *Ecclesiastical History* for King Coelwulf, the cousin of Archbishop Egbert, he was concerned to show a Christian prince his duty towards his people, and he did it by citing examples of failure as well as of success. He told, for instance, the story of the two kings of Essex, Sigehere and Sebbi, who had suffered greatly during the plague of 664. Sigehere

> together with part of his people deserted the sacraments of the Christian faith and apostatised . . . for they loved this present life, seeking no other and not even believing in any future life.

The person who took care to help (since the duty of a prince was the total care of his subjects), was their over-king Wulfhere, who sent Bishop Jaruman to them. He preached with such success that 'they rejoiced to confess the name of Christ which they had denied, choosing rather to die believing that they would rise again in Him'.[5] Now, seventy years later, aware of widespread daily unchecked hypocrisy, freely chosen and not even provoked by hardship, Bede felt that Christianity had been misunderstood as a comforting kind of religion, and Christ as a god of victories, and that therefore the Cross was being seen as a threat and a terror, and not as the very place of redemption; and he warned his colleagues most earnestly against allowing this building on sand to go any further. It was the duty of Bishop Egbert and his cousin King Ceolwulf to reaffirm this Gospel truth, and most of all in the monasteries:

> Protect arduously the flock committed to you from the aud-
> acity of the attacking wolves ... it is your duty to look most
> diligently into what is done righty or wrongly in the monas-
> teries of your diocese ... that the devil may not usurp a
> kingdom for himself in places consecrated to God.[6]

If monastic life especially did not have at its centre the reality of the Cross, it became a source of corruption within the whole of Christian life, and Bede saw that it not only would but should vanish from the earth, a theme echoed by Dom David Knowles, who wrote at the end of his account of monastic life in England and its dissolution nearly a thousand years later:

> Once a religious house or order ceases to direct its sons to
> the abandonment of all that is not God and ceases to show
> them the narrow way that leads to the imitation of Christ in
> his love, it sinks to the level of a purely human institution
> and whatever its works may be they are the works of time
> and not of eternity.[7]

Among other recommendations for meeting the loss of faith among the English, Bede suggested closer study of the book by Gregory the Great called *Pastoral Care*. Bede certainly knew it well, and in his letter to Egbert of York in 734, he described it warmly as

> a remarkable book ... in which the pope sets forth in the
> clearest manner what sort of persons should be chosen to

rule in the church and how these rulers ought to live; and with how much discrimination they ought to instruct different types of listeners and how earnestly they ought each day to reflect on their own frailty.[8]

Now at the end of his life, Bede remembered *Pastoral Care* again:

I urge you to occupy your tongue and your mind with the divine works and with meditation on the scriptures, and especially with reading the letters of the apostle Paul to Timothy and Titus and also the works of the most holy pope Gregory in which he discourses very skilfully concerning the life and vices of rulers in the book of *Pastoral Care* or in the homilies on the Gospels.[9]

Fifty years after Bede's death, the slack and superficial nature of Christianity to which he was drawing attention received its challenge and was found wanting. At the end of the eighth century in England the Cross was applied without palliative and those who had thought Christianity comfortable or consoling found their mistake. Alcuin lamented the sack of Lindisfarne by the Vikings, as a judgement of God on a liberalized Christianity. There is a great deal said today in favour of the Vikings, and an impression exists that they were either fellow-Europeans looking for new trade outlets or well-meaning tourists with long hair who sometimes roughed up the natives. Whatever the hindsight of history has to say about them, the chroniclers of the times were unanimous in their view of them as mad, bad and dangerous to know. It may well have been an error of ignorance when they drank communion wine, raped nuns, burned churches, took away crosses and reliquaries; what they saw was, no doubt, wine, girls, and gold, and wooden churches easily caught fire at a party; but for the Christians, the effect was of sacrilege and the challenge that of martyrdom. How far they failed to meet the challenge in fact and in detail is not my concern, but certainly by 878 Alfred of Wessex was a fugitive king in a land ravaged by 'the heathen men'; the situation was changed by the miracle of the battle of Edington, fought against impossible odds but under the protection of St Mary and St Cuthbert. Alfred's victory and the baptism of Guthrum marked a turning point in the affairs of Christian England. When Alfred looked back over those times he saw that the power of the Cross had crushed rather than sustained those looking for an easy return to peace.

Alfred, the youngest son of Aethelwulf, had succeeded his father and five brothers, all of whom had died fighting the Viking raiders, and had taken on the seemingly hopeless task of defending England against the Danes; he came from a family with high ideals of duty and religion, and in a desperate situation, he did what he saw as his Christian duty before God and his people. He succeeded; the battle of Edington and the baptism of Guthrum marked an end to the Danish attacks and the beginning of that most rare thing, the peaceful cohabitation of two races in one island. It was not just a military success, the practical rallying of men, that made Alfred 'the Great'. Taught by his mother, a devout and thoughtful Christian, he asked himself why God had allowed the Danish devastations of his Christian England which he knew so well from Bede's *Ecclesiastical History*, a book he had caused to be translated into English in his court. The answer was expressed in his preface to his own translation of the *Pastoral Care* of Gregory the Great, and it is significant that it was that book which he translated for his war-torn kingdom. He wrote in the preface:

> I would have it known that very often it has come to my mind what men of learning there were formerly throughout England both in religious and secular orders, and how there were happy times then throughout England.[10]

Learning, he says, declined and 'we were Christians in name alone and very few of us possessed Christian virtues'. Everything, he says, was 'ransacked and burned', but before that, any real understanding of the Christian Gospel had faded out; the ransacking and burning could then be seen not as the hand of God against a gainsaying people but more deeply as the result of culpable lethargy. Genuine contact with the person of Jesus and the reality of the Cross through the Scriptures had disappeared through a lack of energy in acquiring the Latin learning that was a gateway to the Scriptures. So Alfred, like Bede, then asked himself if it would not be better to translate the word of God into a language people understood so that there could be genuine contact with the content of the Gospel again, rather than trying to make the English learn Latin. Alfred was so concerned at the loss of contact with the Gospel that he himself turned his hand to translation with his army still in the field.

I began amidst the various and multifarious afflictions of this kingdom to translate into English the book which in Latin is called the pastoral care, in English 'shepherd book', sometimes word for word, sometimes sense for sense.[11]

Copies were sent to each bishop, as a book 'most necessary for all men to know'. Why was this? It is clear that Alfred regarded the proper task of the Christian leader as attention to the twofold love of God for himself and for others, as described by Gregory; and this was not an ornamental option. It was a vital part of the defence of the realm. For Alfred as for Bede, there was only one way for the English to survive at all, and that was to accept the cross of Christ as the place of resurrection; in other words, having received the Word of the Gospel in the first place, they were committed to living it out to the full; otherwise, they were not just pagans again, but apostates, and therefore all that led to life would lead automatically to death. 'We have now lost wealth as well as wisdom because we did not wish to set our minds in the track.' Such faith began at home, and Alfred appended his own personal prayer to his translation:

Lord God almighty, maker and ruler of all creatures, I beseech you on behalf of your mighty mercy, and through the sign of the holy cross, and through Mary's maidenhood and through Michael's obedience, and through the love and merits of all your saints, that you guide me better than I have done towards you and direct me according to your will and my soul's need better than I myself am able; and strengthen my mind in your will and to my soul's need, and confirm me against the devil's temptations, and keep far from me foul lust and all iniquity; and protect me from my enemies visible and invisible; and teach me to perform your will, that I may inwardly love you before all things with pure thought and clean body, for you are my creator and my redeemer, my sustenance, my consolation, my trust and my hope. Praise and glory be to you now and forever world without end. Amen.[12]

Gregory the apostle of England, faced with the terrors and loneliness of the barbarians' invasions, gave his attention to the responsibility of each Christian to God and to others; Bede, alarmed by the worldliness of his age, recommended Gregory's *Pastoral Care*; Alfred, faced with the Danish invasions, used

Gregory's text for his own bishops and their people. There is here a key to the spirituality of the first English Christians. At first they were promised a new kingdom and tended to see God as the god of battles, who would reward devotion with victory. But they learned another lesson by experience, and that was the priority of God in all circumstances. They were concerned at first with amassing the new glories of the Mediterranean world and an ancient Christian culture; they learned to put first the love of God and the salvation of souls. They learned that belief could not be separated from conduct, and they learned to undertake specific acts of charity not for their own glory but with the humility that regards God as the only pastor, using only damaged tools. The response of these English Christians to personal anguish or to desolation on a tremendous scale lay not in despair or in applying secular solutions to spiritual ills but in the costly assertion that Christ reigns. The answer in both situations was stillness before God to allow him to act: 'Nailed and spread fast on this rood in my holy order as thou wast nailed for me on thy hard rood'.[13] Such stillness is the service that heals. In his book *The Orthodox Way*, Bishop Kallistos quotes a story told by the actress Lillian McCarthy, who went to see George Bernard Shaw when she was distraught with unhappiness:

> I was shivering. Shaw sat very still. The fire brought me no warmth. How long we sat there I do not know but presently I found myself walking with dragging steps with Shaw beside me up and down Adelphi Terrace. The weight upon me grew a little lighter and released the tears which would not come before. He let me cry. Presently I heard a voice in which all the gentleness and tenderness of the world was speaking; it said, 'Look up, dear, look up to the heavens. There is more life than this; there is much more.'[14]

This was the answer to sorrow for the Anglo-Saxons of those early centuries, for the Irish and missionaries from Rome, for Bede and for Cuthbert, for Alfred the Great. In darkness, desolation and shame, in facing the poverty and weakness of the heart, there is the place of the Cross and of the light of life and redemption, because that is the place where God is and no other. If Christianity is true, the only success we know anything about is a man nailed to a cross and still with the Father.

On one of the oldest artefacts of Anglo-Saxon England, the Ruthwell Cross which stood through the Danish raids, is carved the words expanded in the Old English poem *The Dream of the Rood*. The high crosses of Ireland had their counterparts in England. The great stone high crosses at Ruthwell and Bewcastle pre-date the Irish ones that survive, and before those there was almost certainly a similar stone high cross at Jarrow. At Ruthwell in particular, the meaning of the Cross is affirmed by the inscribed runes which form verses from the great Anglo-Saxon poem *The Dream of the Rood*; it epitomizes the love of the Anglo-Saxons for learning to stand where Jesus stands. The meeting-place is the Cross. In the poem, the tree of the Cross is speaking of how it raised up Christ:

> Unclothed Himself God Almighty when he would mount the
>   Cross, courageous in the sight of all men.
> I bore the powerful King, the Lord of heaven; I durst not
>   bend.
> Men mocked us both together. I was bedewed with blood.
> Christ was on the Cross.
> Then I leaned down to the hands of men and they took God
>   Almighty.[15]

> Glory always to God and the Lord our Saviour
> both now and forever,
> while amidst the pressures of adversity
> we still live in the body and are struggling
> since we are away from him,
> and particularly praying
> that the long-desired of all nations shall come
> and deign to enlighten us by the vision of his presence.
> Meanwhile, we deserve to sigh for him
> and earnestly sing,
> because 'one day in your sight
> is better than a thousand'.[16]

Notes

1   Alcuin, 'Letter on the sack of Lindisfarne to Aethelred' in S. Allcott, *Alcuin of York, His Life and Letters* (York, 1974). Letter 12, p. 16.

2   *Anglo-Saxon Chronicle*, trans. N. Garmondsworthy (London, 1975), p. 57.

3   Cuthbert's account of the death of Bede in EHEP, pp. 581–7.

4   Bede, 'Letter to Egbert' in EHEP, trans. with notes J. McClure and R. Collins (Oxford, 1994), pp. 343–57.

5   EHEP, Book 3, cap. xxx, p. 323.

6   'Letter to Egbert', p. 348.

7   David Knowles, *The Religious Orders in England*, vol. III: *The Tudor Age* (Cambridge, 1959), p. 468.

8   EHEP, Book 2 cap. i, p. 127.

9   'Letter to Egbert', p. 344.

10 Alfred, 'Preface to *Pastoral Care*' in *The Age of Alfred*, trans. S. Keynes and M. Lapidge (Harmondsworth, 1983), p. 124.

11 Ibid., p. 125.

12 Ibid., p. 137.

13 *A Talking of the Love of God*, ed. M. S. Westra (The Hague, 1950), p. 58.

14 Quoted in Kallistos Ware, *The Orthodox Way* (Oxford, 1979), p. 54.

15 Cf. Eamonn O'Carragain, 'The Ruthwell crucifixion poem and its iconographic and liturgical contexts', *Peritia: Journal of the Medieval Academy of Ireland*, vi–vii, pp. 1–71, 187–8. Also *The Ruthwell Cross*, ed. Brendan Cassidy (Princeton, NJ, 1992).

16 Bede, *Commentary on the Seven Catholic Epistles*, trans. D. Hurst (Kalamazoo, 1985), Commentary on 1 Peter 3.18, p. 156.

Further reading

Most of these titles are in addition to books referred to in the notes. References to Bede's works are either to translations into English or to the critical edition of his works published in *Corpus Christianorum Series Latina*, (Turnhout: Brepols) by volume and page number.

A. Bede

Bede, *Ecclesiastical History of the English People*, ed. and trans. B. Colgrave and R. A. B. Mynors (Oxford, 1969).

Ecclesiastical History of the English People, ed. J. McClure and R. Collins (World Classics Series, 1994).

C. Plummer, *Venerabilis Baedae Historiam Ecclesiasticam Gentia Anglorum* (2 vols; Oxford, 1896) (reprinted 1954). Latin text with admirable and copious notes in English.

J. M. Wallace-Hadrill, *Bede's Ecclesiastical History of the English People* (Oxford, 1988) (notes to the EHEP).

English Historical Documents, vol. 1; *c*. 500–1041, ed. D. Whitelock (Oxford/New York, 1979).

Bede, *Life of St Cuthbert*, ed. and trans. B. Colgrave, *Two Lives of St Cuthbert* (Cambridge, 1940).

Bede, *On the Tabernacle*, trans. A. Holder (Liverpool, 1994).

Bede, *On the Temple*, trans. Sean Connolly (Liverpool, 1995).

Homilies of the Venerable Bede, trans. L. Martin and D. Hurst, 2 vols (Kalamazoo, 1991).
The Age of Bede, ed. D. Farmer (Harmondsworth, 1980).
Life of Ceolfrid, trans. D. S. Boutflower (London, 1912).

B. Other Early Sources

Adamnan, *Life of St Columba*, ed. R. Sharpe (Penguin Classics, 1981).
Aldhelm, *The Prose Works*, ed. M. Lapidge and M. Herren (Cambridge, 1979).
Alfred the Great, ed. S. Keynes (Harmondsworth, 1985).
Anglo-Saxon Poetry, ed. A. J. Bradley (London, 1982).
Earliest Life of St Gregory the Great, ed. and trans. B. Colgrave (Kansas, 1968).
Eddius Stephanus, *Life of Bishop Wilfrid*, ed. and trans. B. Colgrave (Cambridge, 1956).
The Life of St Guthlac of Crowland, ed. and trans. B. Colgrave (Cambridge, 1956).

C. Modern Works

H. Barre, *Prières anciennes de l'Occident à la Mère du Sauveur* (Paris, 1963).
P. Hunter Blair, *Northumbria in the Age of Bede* (London, 1976).
The Anglo Saxons, ed. James Campbell (Oxford, 1982).
M. T. A. Carroll, *The Venerable Bede: His Spiritual Teachings* (Washington, 1946).
Douglas Dales, *Light to the Isles* (Cambridge, 1997).
M. Deansley, *The Pre-Conquest Church in England* (London, 1961).
M. L. W. Laistner, *Thought and Letters in Western Europe, 500–900* (London, 1957).
H. Mayr-Harting, *The Coming of Christianity to Anglo-Saxon England* (London, 1972).
Barbara Raw, *Anglo-Saxon Crucifixion Iconography and the Art of the Monastic Revival* (Cambridge, 1990).
Bede: Life, Times and Writings, ed. A. H. Thompson (London 1935).
Benedicta Ward, *The Venerable Bede* (London, 1981)

Benedicta Ward, *Bede and the Psalter* (Jarrow, 1981).

Famulus Christi: Essays in Commemoration of the Thirteenth Centenary of the Venerable Bede, ed. Gerald Bonner (London, 1976).

St Cuthbert, His Cult and His Community, ed. G. Bonner, D. W. Rollason and C. Stancliffe (London, 1989).

Index

INDEX